# *You* DESERVE MORE

# JEWEL DIAMOND TAYLOR

# You
# DESERVE
# MORE

YOU DESERVE MORE

A New Spirit Novel

ISBN-13: 978-0-373-83155-5
ISBN-10:      0-373-83155-2

**Printed in U.S.A.**

## Acknowledgment

I am a diamond with flaws and yet God sent me
earthly angels to love me.

Family and friends truly bless and enrich my life in so many ways.
The circle of love that surrounds me gives me room to grow and
share my gems of inspiration through the spoken word and the
pen. I love you.

Thank you to my husband, John, and my sons
John and Jason Taylor.
My loving sisters: Jamila Holloway and Joy Lewis.
My sisterfriends: Kathi Arnold, Aliyah Azziz, Toni Burton,
Judith Clark, Deborah Granger, CeCe Gray, Kym Richards,
Julia Shaw, Carolyn Washington, Paula Watts and Angie Westfield.
My Goddaughters: Toi Arnold, Dwanda Gossett,
Rochelle Hall and Dawn Harvey.
My brotherfriends: Tracy Kennedy, Victor McGlothin
and Lionel Woodyard.
Your light, love, loyalty, laughs and learning lessons cause
my soul to expand and rejoice.
Collectively, you have all been the wind beneath my wings.

Thank you, Maria Dowd. Because of your invitation and support,
I traveled with you for twelve years as one of your speakers and as
mistress of ceremonies for a phenomenal journey with the
African American Women on Tour conferences (AAWOT). This
opportunity increased my visibility and enlarged my networking
opportunities. The sisterfriends from AAWOT have blessed me
with memories that will last for a lifetime.

Thank you to all of the women who attend my Women on the
Grow conferences and retreats. All of you ladies have allowed me to
grow and polish up my women's ministry skills. I am honored and
blessed to serve you.

Thank you, to all of my fans, readers, clients, customers and
prayer warriors. I wish I could remember and include ALL
your names. Gratitude is forever in my heart for you.

Thank you, Bishop Kenneth C. Ulmer, Sr. Pastor of
Faithful Central Bible Church, for being so instrumental
in my spiritual growth.

# ❧ TABLE OF CONTENTS ❧

# ❧ INTRODUCTION ❧

It is so amazing to think how we as women lose so much time, money, self-respect and peace of mind because we are hurting, lonely, weak, broken and in large part have a low Relationships IQ. I've had some hard lessons to learn in discovering my own value and voice. Because of what I have lost and given away, I have now gained new divine insight. At the risk of being exposed, judged, ridiculed and misunderstood, I have exchanged my shame and brokenness for my Lord's salvation and peace of mind. Yes, in my former years I was lost and found with low self-esteem, modeling the behavior of my passive mother. My precious mother passed on to Glory before she could pass on pearls of wisdom about relationships, dating and marriage. She never learned them, so how could I expect her to teach me? When I realized this, I stopped blaming her and began my journey of healing. I did receive lots of nurturing from my mother, Aunt Janet and sisters.

Through my healing journey to be a whole woman with self-esteem and a smart heart, I realized I always had mother nurturing, but I lacked affirmation and attention from my biological father and stepfather. I had no brothers and little interaction with men to understand their mysteries, communication dynamics and games. The presence or the absence of a father in a daughter's life really shape, mold and educate her with a high Relationships IQ. My biological father was not physically available for my daddy's-girl training because of my parents' divorce when I was seven. My later stepfather was a good provider but never emotionally available for me or my two younger sisters. But I discovered there are father-daughter stories in the Bible (e.g., Jairus and his daughter; Phillip and his four daughters). These are positive stories that offer healing for daughters wounded by fathers.

Dancing with your father, talking with your father, hugs from your father, learning how to interact with other men and learning resiliency through adversity are great gifts many of us never received from our fathers. Even though I have never gained the affirmation, strength and love that I craved from my earthly fathers or uncles, I have learned to know the depth, compassion and power of my heavenly Father's love.

Even though the message in this book sounds the alarm for women to be aware of mistreatment and heartache, this is not about male bashing. There are good men and fathers with good hearts.

And there are men who have actually told me before they became mature and righteous men how they used to prey on and seek out weak women. Men have said in my workshops (laughing as they told their stories) how they could spot a sucker in the crowd. They admitted that giving a compliment, a little attention and manipulation got them what they wanted. A brother in the printing office saw me working on one of my books and told me I was the enemy to those type of men because I was enlightening and empowering women to open their eyes.

It's sad but true…desperation and weakness are something dishonorable men can detect. When a woman allows the scent of man and sex to take over her good sense, she will eventually have a broken heart. So this book is simply my contribution to the healing and awareness needed to open women's eyes. When we know better…we can do better. I want to be a part of the solution. I have certainly made some foolish choices in the past. I don't have all the answers. You may not agree with all my ideas. My intention here is to share what I have learned and experienced from my own growth and from counseling with other women.

Because of my own awakening and the grace of God in my life, I feel compelled to put to paper some relationship lessons. If you identify with any of the issues discussed, don't beat yourself up with shame. You're not alone. My prayer is that these messages serve as a healing balm and a rope to pull you out of the quicksand of any unhealthy relationship. You will need to read the book several times before you are able to accept and internalize new relationship skills.

Come on…tell the truth. Are you now or have you ever been desperate in the past and caught up in a mesmerizing relationship that had no future? Or have you seen the foolish and desperate things another woman has done just to get the attention of a man or to hang on to the one she had. Isn't it sad?

Sisters, daughters, mothers, grandmothers and friends… we have work to do. We have to break some generational cycles of depression, suicide, divorce, desperation, broken hearts and our children learning unhealthy relationship skills. We can sometimes be smart with our heads but *not* with our hearts.

Be sure to pass this book along to your daughter, your coworker sitting next to you, your best friend, that sister at church who is reaching out for help, or even your mother. This is excellent material to share at a women's retreat or study group. It's crucial to understand that your emotional scars, beliefs, memories, music, media, role models, romance myths and your sense of worth are powerful forces shaping your behavior. These determine who you allow into your heart, spirit and bedroom. What you don't know can hurt you. We must grow, share and pray for God's mercy, grace and direction in our lives. Some of us have the victory now over immature, reckless and sinful relationships. Nothing will change for us until we are able to tell the truth to ourselves and tell our stories of desperation and deliverance. Education leads to liberation.

This small yet powerful book promises to increase your Relationships IQ. Read this message often to teach your heart to be smart. As you read the uplifting material in each chapter, you are encouraged to reflect on the bible verses and affirmations, then write your thoughts and prayers on the journal pages. Let the truth set you free.

—*Jewel Diamond Taylor*

# CHAPTER 1

## RELATIONSHIPS IQ

So many women have an intense desire to be loved, affirmed, cherished and married. Women too often think and assume that he wants the same thing she wants. We want a relationship to work out just the way we picture it in our minds. We get these fantasies frozen in our minds from images in movies, songs and fairy tales like *Cinderella*, *Sleeping Beauty*, *Sleepless in Seattle* and *How Stella Got Her Groove Back*. These seemingly harmless happy-ending images create tunnel vision, which blocks out reality. Rushing into emotional or sexual intimacy causes us to fast-forward and skip over the real process of building a relationship based on time, dating, trust, communication, asking qualifying questions, honesty, disciplining our hormones, shared values, boundaries and friendship. Because of tunnel vision you don't see red flags. That's why people say love is blind. Well, that's true when your hormones are raging, your Relationships IQ is low and your neediness and loneliness are giving off the scent of desperation. If you were to see a counselor, your pastor or me, the "Self-esteem Doctor," we would tell you that you are wearing a "pink lens." When you are lovesick and desperate, you are not seeing clearly. You are idolizing and exaggerating his virtues and minimizing his flaws.

You think in your mind that you both connected in some way and that you have a relationship. You see what you want to see. When love is blind, you don't see his or your own issues, flaws, romance-addiction patterns, lust or immaturity. You don't see the betrayal, breakup or divorce coming.

Lovesickness can make you blind and deaf. You don't hear your inner voice or acknowledge the cautions and wisdom of family, friends and elders.

You don't hear the Lord's word hidden in your spirit. You don't hear what He is saying or, most important, what He is not saying. You only hear what you need to hear. Oh, I know, honey…this message can sting. Don't stop, continue to read on.

Sometimes I laugh and sometimes I just shake my head as I remember all the times I was naive, immature and wearing my pink glasses. My heart has not always been smart. Even at this seasoned age of being a wife, mother, an elder, spiritual counselor, speaker and author, I still remember how it feels to be lovesick. It is not a pretty sight. I would remember one little statement and hold on to it in my heart's memory forever. I can still remember whispers in my ears, while dancing in the dark, on the phone, across the dinner table, in the movies, in the back-seat of a car or while what I thought was making love... but it was just lust.

I truly know what it is to be smart in my head and yet stupid with my heart choices. Through my own on-going healing, increasing my Relationships IQ, prayers, forgiveness and salvation from the Lord, I now possess a secret strength. I can truly say I know about God's favor, mercy and grace... Allelujah!

Desperation is a terrible fragrance to wear. You're wearing the scent of despair and low self-esteem when you cling, obsess and beg someone to love you and stay with you when he can't return the love you deserve.

In the movies falling in love = marriage. In real life, falling in love or a long-term relationship does not always result in marriage. When pain and loss happen in your life, you can either choose to suffer and feel like a victim or learn the lessons of life and love. Learning and maturing from each life lesson gives you a secret strength.

Let it go, dear, so your heart and spirit can heal. Don't dial those digits. Don't circle his house. Don't blow up his cell phone all day with desperate messages. Don't fill up his voice mail and e-mail box with sad messages. Don't put your life on hold. Don't neglect yourself, your family, your dreams, your goals or your faith.

No one person is responsible for your happiness. You don't ever want to give someone that much power. Never make someone a priority, who has made you an option.

Sometimes what we think is rejection…is really God's protection pointing us in a new direction.

Open your eyes and see your real worth and beauty in the mirror. Get balance in your life. Get help from the wise women in your life. Pour all that misguided and untapped passion into your goals and dreams.

When your heart is smart you can avoid the pitfalls, anxiety and pain of living in a chaotic, drama-filled, sitting-by-the-phone, life-on-hold and stressful world.

Increase your Relationships IQ by knowing these important points and recognizing the potential traps:

**Am I Needy?**—I can't stand to be alone; I accept less than what I'm worth because it's better than being alone; I hear myself saying, "Call me, do you love me?…I don't know what to do, help me, save me, you're stronger than me."

**Am I Naive?**—I ignore the red flags waving that he is not the one. I continue to ignore his lateness, his rudeness, his addictions, those strange phone calls, loan him too much money, he's always having a crisis, I can never find him, I make excuses and rationalize his temper and abuse, I think I can change him even though I see signs that he is immature, gay, bisexual, married, in between relationships, can't keep a job, won't talk, I don't read enough materials to increase my Relationships IQ, etc.

**Am I Desperate?**—When love walks out the door and doesn't answer your phone calls anymore, do you start drowning in the pool of what's wrong with me?—It must be my fault—I can't believe he doesn't see how good I am for him—How could he change so fast?—I can't breathe without him?

That kind of emotional agony makes you lovesick and desperate.

Did you ever notice that there are many cold and cruel lyrics on the music charts written for a woman who can't let go and gave her all to a relationship or marriage. Or maybe she thought she just thought she was in a "relationship" that really didn't exist. Either way, the truth hurts. When someone can't return your love, it hurts like hell. A love hangover keeps you confused, bewildered, depressed and damages your sense of worth.

- ◆ If love isn't lifting you up, it ain't love!
- ◆ If love doesn't come home, it ain't love!
- ◆ If love doesn't return your calls, it ain't love!
- ◆ If your life is on hold and you can't eat, sleep, work, study or pray, it ain't love!
- ◆ If love isn't loving you, stop in the name of love.
- ◆ Love yourself before you give your heart and soul away again.

It's unfortunate that wounded people either give up on themselves, and give up on ever being loved again. If this is you...don't give up. Love will come again.

♥ *Remember, diamonds only sparkle because they go under pressure, through the fire and polishing. Be like a diamond and let your light shine.*

Generally speaking, men tend to rush into physical intimacy. Many women rush into emotional intimacy. Men like to share *information* but a woman sometimes thinks that communicating is about talking about *feelings*. She wants to talk and share all of her dreams, secrets, and eventually her vulnerabilities are exposed. And eventually it could drive a man away who is not able or ready for emotional intimacy.

In the early stages of a new relationship, if a woman is too needy and desperate, she may give too much and give too soon. If she feels unworthy and suffers from low self-esteem, she may feel she has to earn love.

She lives with hopeless devotion and is willing to wait. Therefore, she may try to buy love by being too available, too accommodating and overcompensating with gifts, sex, running errands, paying for the date, paying his bills and more, just to prove her love.

Generally speaking, men do not think about relationships as much as women. Men are socialized to master work, wages, war and women. Yes, men are passionate, but about different things than women. Men tend to be more passionate about their careers, sports, money, sex and cars. Their attention, thoughts, conversations and energy tend to focus on those things first. Don't take it personally.

Just get wise and understand that men and women are wired and socialized differently. The male and female define their power, image and worth from different stimuli and circumstances. Once you understand this, you won't find yourself assuming that his every waking moment is about you, your relationship and where it is going.

Just like dogs can smell fear, anyone without virtue will recognize a weak and needy person and take advantage of their vulnerability.

Desperation is an invisible quality. It's an aura that a person can sense through your behavior, words and tolerance of bad behavior.

A good man who really cares and respects you would not take advantage of you. If you are wearing the perfume of desperation, an unworthy man can smell it. Unfortunately, he will misuse your body, time, money and heart.

Being needy, naive, desperate and having low expectations will surely cause you heartache and pain.

You may fall in love with someone's personality, but it's his character you really live with.

You deserve more than:

+ a part-time love
+ a "booty call"
+ shared love
+ secret love
+ "I love you if" kind of love
+ abusive love (emotional or physical)
+ a date with only fast food and fast sex

♥ *Start believing you are whole and okay whether
you are in a relationship or not.*

You may wake up thinking about him and he wakes up
thinking about how much money he can make today or
where is the game or who and where he will satisfy his
sexual urges and fantasies.

Men who have options don't necessarily think that
sleeping together means you're in a serious relationship.
Once you have gotten sexually intimate with a man, your
heart is in…your heart is open and asking questions that
he doesn't have answers for.

When your heart is not smart, you could find yourself
wanting the emotional intimacy. You want to move
quickly after the attraction stage to the bonding stage
(i.e., attachment, comfort, familiarity, routine).

The initial attraction stage is fun. It's the honeymoon
or what I call the "magical dust" stage. When a woman
moves too quickly and falls too deeply, the more distant
the man is likely to become. I don't know the magical
formula and time line to move into each new level. Each
individual and circumstance is different. It's a challenge
and learning lesson to know how to stay on the same page
as you both learn to know each other. A relationship has
a better chance if you can learn to "grow" in love instead
of *falling* in love.

Women can act too strong and give too much to her
man to cover up her feelings of inadequacy or her unspoken assumptions of commitment and a future.

Women can act too weak, dependent and helpless, giving her man all the power to make him feel more important.

Giving too much to your man can make him too lazy and he loses interest or he will take, take and take. Why?...because he has gotten used to being the receiver and loses interest in pursuing and providing for you.

As women, we need to learn emotional fitness and strengthen our Relationships IQ because our feelings can be our worst enemy or best friend.

Whether the man in your life is a friend, lover or husband, men like women who like themselves. Women who have very low self-esteem are dangerous. Men think they are hysterical, stalkers, whiners, weak and needy.

The pursuing and providing nature of a man determines the degree of his masculinity, power and identity. Men measure their masculinity by what they can do, possess and conquer, not necessarily always by relationships.

Too often, women find themselves acting the role of mother with her mate. She's paying the bills, cleaning up, making all the decisions, rescuing him from trouble and then one day she explodes with anger or illness after so many years because she is resentful, stressed and unappreciated.

What are you letting your partner get away with just so you can say you have a man? Do you find yourself continually adjusting, accommodating and compromising to keep the relationship or to avoid fights, black eyes or withdrawal of affection or money?

When you are giving too much, you become what I call an "emotional bellhop," because you are carrying a heavy bag of emotions.

Erykah Badu wrote a popular song that gave us a new term called "bag lady." Her lyrical metaphors empower women. She advises women to guard their hearts against pain and lightly pack their emotions.

Desperate, lonely and enabling women too often carry heavy emotional baggage of grief, sadness, depression, desperation, low self-esteem and suicidal thoughts.

Bag ladies are the walking wounded, haunted by the questions "Why did he leave me? ...What's wrong with me? ...I don't want to be alone? ...Why did he choose her over me? ...I'm not complete without him ...Who is he with now? ...I love him–I hate him ...I want revenge ...I want him back."

You can't breathe, live or be happy carrying all that junk. Let it go, sisters.

Don't become a professional "emotional bellhop" carrying all that toxic and heavy stuff everywhere you go. No matter what your status is, and what type of bag you carry, budget priced or designer, all you need to hold on to is you.

Sometimes women love so strongly and passionately that they get caught up in an emotional and tumultuous affair. When the love you are receiving raises warning signals, you could be in a toxic relationship. Genuine love will not leave you feeling depressed, insecure and abused. Spend some time with yourself and recognize these signs; this knowledge could save you a lot of future heartache.

Here is a short list of the characteristics of genuine love vs. toxic love:

GENUINE LOVE　Compromise, negotiation or taking turns at leading. Problem solving together.

TOXIC LOVE　Power plays for control; blaming; passive or aggressive manipulation.

GENUINE LOVE　Embracing each other's individuality.

TOXIC LOVE　Trying to change other to own image.

GENUINE LOVE　Relationship deals with all aspects of reality.

TOXIC LOVE　Relationship is based on delusion and avoidance of the unpleasant.

GENUINE LOVE　Self-care by both partners; emotional state not dependent on other's mood.

TOXIC LOVE　Expectation that one partner will fix and rescue the other.

GENUINE LOVE　Loving detachment (healthy concern about partner, while letting go).

TOXIC LOVE　Fusion (being obsessed with each other's problems and feelings).

GENUINE LOVE　Sex is free choice growing out of caring and friendship.

TOXIC LOVE　Pressure around sex due to insecurity, fear and need for immediate gratification.

GENUINE LOVE  Ability to enjoy being alone.
TOXIC LOVE  Unable to endure separation; clinging.

GENUINE LOVE  Cycle of comfort and contentment.
TOXIC LOVE  Cycle of pain and despair.

GENUINE LOVE  Development of self first priority.
TOXIC LOVE  Obsession with relationship.

GENUINE LOVE  Room to grow, expand; desire for other to grow.
TOXIC LOVE  Intensity of need seen as proof of love (may really be fear, insecurity, loneliness).

GENUINE LOVE  Separate interests; other friends; maintain other meaningful relationships.
TOXIC LOVE  Total involvement; limited social life; neglect old friends and interests.

GENUINE LOVE  Encouragement of each other's expanding; secure in own worth.
TOXIC LOVE  Preoccupation with other's behavior; fear of other changing.

GENUINE LOVE  Appropriate trust (i.e., trusting partner to behave according to fundamental nature).
TOXIC LOVE  Jealousy; possessiveness; fear of competition; overprotective and territorial.

Yes, life can hurt and life is beautiful.

Surviving and being resourceful through tough times breeds confidence.

Trusting God through the rough times breeds faith.

*Now faith is the substance of things hoped for, the evidence of things not seen.*

—Hebrews 11:1

When someone is desperate, they don't know how to establish emotional boundaries to keep the drama, abuse, disrespect, lies and confusion OUT of their life. Growing in a sense of wholeness and worthiness will help you distance yourself with emotional boundaries. Once you allow these negative emotions and habits into your life, your emotional guard is down.

Don't let the negative into your circle of life. Strengthen your boundaries. Fight temptation.

It wants to come into your life and take over.

Temptation whispers your name and keeps you caught up in a game you can't win. Ask for help.

Be especially alert against the beginnings of temptation, for the enemy is more easily conquered if he is refused admittance to the mind and is met at the door with faith, discipline, courage and a made-up mind. Someone once said, "If you don't want to slip, stay away from the slippery places."

## Signs and Symptoms of "Desperation"

Addictive attachment, the blues, carelessness, downheartedness, dreariness, hopelessness, melancholy, misery, pain, sadness, sorrow, trouble, unhappiness, caught up in the constant search for a partner, the endless intrigue of flirtations, sexual liaisons and affairs leaving a path of destruction and negative consequences, seeking a new romantic affair or liaison, growing steadily more unhappy, fearful and bored and ends up pushing their partner away or looking outside the relationship for yet another new intensity or "love" like a romantic fix and high, constantly seeking a sexual partner, new romance or significant other, an inability or difficulty in being alone, consistently choosing partners who are abusive or emotionally unavailable, using sex, seduction and intrigue to "hook" or hold on to a partner, using sex or romantic intensity to tolerate difficult experiences or emotions, missing out on important family, career or social experiences in order to maintain a sexual high or romantic relationship, an inability to leave unhealthy relationships despite repeated promises to self or others, returning to previously unmanageable or painful relationships despite promises to self or others, mistaking sexual experiences, romantic "high" and rendezvous for love.

♥ *Stop buying tickets for those emotional roller-coaster rides.*

You can't make someone love you or make someone stay. If you develop self-esteem, spiritual discernment and "a life," you won't find yourself making someone else responsible for your happiness or responsible for your pain.

Manipulation, control, jealousy, neediness and selfishness are not the ingredients of a thriving, healthy, loving and lasting relationship.

Seeking status, sex, wealth and security are the wrong reasons to be in a relationship.

The following qualities build a strong foundation: communication, intimacy, trust, a sense of humor, sharing household tasks, some getaway time without business or children, forgiveness, daily exchanges of:

a meal, a hug, a call, a touch, a note, leaving a nice message on voice mail, sharing common goals and interests, creating and sharing a spiritual foundation to grow through adversity and experience prosperity.

Don't allow other people to control, manipulate or validate your existence. Value your dreams, body, goals, time and peace of mind. If you don't...no one else will.

♥ *A kiss isn't a promise. Sex doesn't equal love.*

Nobody can take away your pain,
so don't let anyone take away your happiness.

Do not ask God to guide your feet
if you are not willing to move your feet.

*In the day of prosperity be joyful, but in the day of adversity consider.*

—Ecclesiastes 7:14

Being criticized and misunderstood
will happen in life.

Don't be discouraged.

Around every flower are insects.

They still open up, bloom and grow.
They understand insects will come
because of their aroma, color and beauty.

Don't stop growing because of the
"insects" in your life.

*Therefore my beloved, be steadfast, immovable,
always excelling in the work of the Lord...*
—1 Corinthians 15:58

# JOURNAL PAGE

_____

_____

_____

_____

_____

_____

_____

_____

_____

_____

# JOURNAL PAGE

# CHAPTER 2

## THE FOUNDATION OF RELATIONSHIPS

*Who Taught You About Relationships?*

Society, media and the music industry promote and perpetuate the idea of romance, quick-fix solutions, "celebrity couples" and the myth of the "beautiful" people in fairy tales. We live in a culture of image, reality shows and "sex in the city." We are measured by how good we look, how much we have, and if we have someone by our side that supports a good image. We have, sadly, been socialized to look outside ourselves for happiness and love. Our obsession with love pervades every aspect of popular culture, from novels to hip-hop and pop-song lyrics, and even great works of poetry, drama and art. Our culture idealizes, dramatizes and models a dependency that says we cannot live without another person, sex or romance.

A woman tends to center her life around relationships, while men tend to center their priorities around work, money, power and status. As little girls, we were being prepared for relationships playing with dolls, reading bridal magazines and reading fairy tales with happy endings. We were talking, crying, laughing, playing, dreaming, studying and in some cases pampered or in worst cases...hurt, abused and violated by men.

Little boys were fighting, reading "girlie" magazines, experimenting with sex, missing class and playing games. A lot of them learned how to be players on and off the field. Unfortunately, little boys and little girls too often grow up unprepared for intimate relationships. We learn about relationships from examples, experience and education.

Our parents are our first role models and we unconsciously seek them again in our relationships.

If you idolized your parents and felt protected and loved by them, you are mystified by them. If this mystification is really deep, it can set you up to have unrealistic expectations of your mate.

If your parents were physically or emotionally absent or if you witnessed abuse, neglect, infidelity and reckless sexual behavior, you weren't provided with good examples to know what healthy love looks like.

When women are unconsciously seeking a daddy, "someone to watch over me, protect me, love me and provide for me"...she could potentially find herself in desperate situations where she is being controlled and treated like a child instead of a cherished adult.

Behaving in desperate ways and lowering expectations

and standards in your relationship can be an unconscious attempt to satisfy your hunger for security, sensation, power, belonging, attention and meaning. You may have unresolved feelings of "never having enough" or "not being enough."

Do you have any positive relationships around you modeling healthy and loving examples of two people who have respect, affection, loyalty, communication, forgiveness, a sense of humor, mutual support, shared interests, love, trust, cooperation and spirituality?

Let's check your emotional temperature. Imagine you are sitting in the Self-esteem Doctor's office and you are being asked:

❑ Do you find yourself losing sleep and can't think clearly for long periods of time after you meet a new love interest?

❑ Do you get addicted to the euphoric effects of romance?

❑ Do you find it difficult to let go of a toxic relationship even when you are unhappy, depressed, lonely, neglected or in danger?

❑ Do you give too much or take too much abuse and neglect in the hope that he will not leave or that someday he will marry you?

❑ Do you obsess about someone who is unavailable? Are you suffering in silence?

❑ Are you a torch bearer addicted to fantasies, illusions and unavailable men?

❑ Are you involved with someone who only offers "romance" meaning sexual passion and pseudo emotional intimacy? Does your partner offer the highs of romance without any commitment or bonding with you? Is he there for you when it really counts? Or are you just his playmate?

❑ Do you have weak personality boundaries with your partner and secretly hope he will change?

❑ Do you exchange your own identity with your partner, reacting to your partner's problems as if they were your own?

❑ Do you crave his love to make you feel whole?

❑ Do you always hear about his excuses and how he is *so* busy that he doesn't have time for you?

❑ Do you spend too much time waiting, guessing, wondering and suspicious about his loyalty and love for you?

❑ Do you become totally involved in the other person, neglecting your own life, social circle and interests? Are you so preoccupied with him that you abandon your family, friends, work and school for this relationship?

❑ Do you panic at the thought of losing him?

❑ Do you find yourself lying to cover up for your partner?

❑ Do you constantly lend money that your partner doesn't pay back?

❑ Are you always bailing your partner out of trouble?

❑ Do you only have his cell phone number and can never reach him at his home or job?

❑ Does your partner keep secrets and lies about fidelity, past marriages, children, addictions, spending habits, criminal activity or past jobs?

❑ Do you rely on the courts, the police and trusted friends to help you with your partner's destructive behavior?

❑ Do you believe that if the obvious problems disappeared, your relationship would be perfect?

❑ Are you looking for those highs; that buzz provided by new relationships (i.e., candlelight dinners and romantic cards; boxes of chocolates, weekend getaways, long sweet phone calls)? These quick highs are mood altering, which can get you hooked and soon have you experiencing a love hangover.

❑ Do you rush into sexual intimacy without protection or commitment?

❑ Do you fall in love too easily not realizing he is not really that into you?

❑ Do you think having sex equals love?

❑ Do you think having sex means you have a relationship?

❑ Are you involved with a man even though you know he is dating someone else, married or still living at home with his parents?

❑ Do you believe you can make him happy even though he is telling you that he won't leave his wife and children?

❑ Are you secretive about your relationship?

❑ Are you caught up in a fantasy because of his looks, image, income or status?

❏ Do you introduce your children and family to someone you don't have enough information about?

❏ Do you know vital information about the man you're dating or about to marry? (Social-security number, credit rating, any criminal record, do you know his family and friends, do you know about his health status, do you know his spending habits, do you know about his faith, are you aware of any business or financial arrangements with his ex-wife, children, business obligations, investments, etc.?)

❏ Are you putting your children at risk by moving a man into your home that you don't know well and someone who is not married to you?

❏ Do you try to save, protect or help too much, trying to control things your partner should be doing, e.g., looking up classified ads to find him a job, pay bills, help his children, etc.?

Falling in and out of love can make you dizzy. It's a sign that you are addicted to some crazy love. Maybe it really isn't love. Some people just like the idea of being in love.

If you're in and out of love, stop and check yourself. If you're constantly falling...is that love? If love is bringing you down, it ain't love! If love doesn't respect you, it ain't love! If love ignores your calls, it ain't love! If your life is on hold and you are discouraged in seeking higher education, climbing the ladder in your career, and in trying to have a better life for yourself, it ain't love.

You need to learn to love yourself first in order to get the right kind of love.

When dating, make sure you're both looking for the same thing. Sometimes people are not seeking their soulmate or a helpmate...just a playmate.

♥ *Physical attraction creates desire. Mental attraction creates interest. Emotional attraction creates affection. Spiritual attraction creates love.*

That great boyfriend may not be the best choice for you as a husband. Your expectations may be different.

Take your time and ask the right questions:

> In the movies, falling in love seems to always end in marriage.
>
> In real life, falling in love does *not* always lead to marriage.
>
> Women expect it and men know that, so they close their hearts.

♦ Is this relationship about love or lust?

♦ Is this relationship full of drama and deceit?

♦ Does this person want the same things in life that I value?

♦ Am I on the rebound trying to forget my last relationship?

♦ Am I chasing or am I choosing?

♦ Am I so afraid of being alone that I settle for less, mess and stress?

♦ Is he here only for the good times and I can't find him when the going gets tough?

♦ Has the thrill gone, but neither one of us wants to be the first to say goodbye?

♦ Am I experiencing *Deja-fool,* repeating the same issues...same script...but a different cast?

You can make yourself sick, angry and depressed if you constantly think and debate about the outcomes in your life that cannot be changed or controlled.

Make a list of the things you *can* change. Start there with some action and a plan. If you continue to whine, wait, worry, weep and wish things were better...you only lose time and energy. Instead of telling God about your big problems...tell your problems that you have a big God.

Everyday I am learning how to be responsible
and proactive in my choices.

I trust myself to do what is best for my life.

*But thanks be to God, who in Christ always leads us
in triumphal procession, and through us spreads in
every place the fragrance that comes from knowing
Him.*

—2 Corinthians 2:14

Even when the path seems unclear,
I am empowered to do great things.
I trust myself to make decisions.
I believe that God lives in me
and orders my steps.

*You chart the path ahead of me and tell me where to
stop and rest. Every moment you know where I am.
You both precede and follow me.*

*You place your hand of blessing on my head. I can
never escape from your Spirit. I can never get away
from your presence…your strength will support me.*
—Psalms 139:3, 5,10

# JOURNAL PAGE

_____

_____

_____

_____

_____

_____

_____

_____

_____

_____

# JOURNAL PAGE

_____

_____

_____

_____

_____

_____

_____

_____

_____

_____

_____

# CHAPTER

## EMOTIONAL INTELLIGENCE

3

The two major emotional voids that women usually try to fill are feeling incomplete or feeling unhappy. If you've been hurt, criticized or unloved, don't make stupid choices to fill up the emptiness in your life. It's important to develop healthy emotional intelligence.

> If you neglect yourself, others will learn to neglect you.
>
> The way you treat yourself teaches others how to treat you.

I categorize *wounded women* into two profiles.

The **type P** woman is passive, needy or naive. This profile is more prone to be depressed and desperate in relationships where she is dominated or even abused (emotionally or physically).

The opposite extreme is the **type S** woman, who becomes fiercely independent because of trust issues. The **type S** woman uses words and body language that repel relationships.

This wounded profile becomes so self-sufficient, suspicious of others and skeptical in love and faith. Her heart is hard and closed. However, the **type P** woman has a heart that is too trusting and open. As women, we must be smart and strive for a balance to avoid becoming so extreme in our behavior and beliefs.

Denial, depression and destructive habits can rob you of peace, health and a fulfilling life. Love yourself enough to take back your personal power to recover your self-esteem and discover the quality of life you deserve.

What usually happens is that we fall in love and then we fall into reality. Every relationship has issues to work through, pray through and overcome.

| I | Illusions (denial, false expectations, perpetuated media stereotypes and romance myths, fairy tales with happy endings) |
|---|---|
| S | Sex (sexual/intimacy compatibility, infidelity) |
| $ | Money habits (credit, salary, employment, shopping, gambling, supporting other family members) |
| U | Unfinished business (divorce, child support, rebound love, criminal record, etc.) |
| E | Emotional baggage (anger, bitterness, trust issues from the past, immaturity, depression, childhood trauma, addictions) |
| S | Spiritual values (do you both share the same faith?) |

If you are desperate and impulsive, you may be blind to these issues. You could find yourself trying to fix or rescue someone. Or your fear and loss of self-respect could make you try to change and lose yourself in an effort to hold on to a bad relationship.

The more experienced and whole person with emotional boundaries has a better chance of avoiding painful, stressful and costly relationships. This person is also more capable of coping with the eventual disappointments and issues that need to be resolved to maintain a relationship.

♥ *Be prepared to experience everything from boredom to ecstasy, joy and pain, sickness and health, compliments and criticism, devotion and disappointments. Relationships are where the little boy or little girl in both of you continues to grow up. Don't allow illusions and unrealistic expectations to distort your thinking and behavior.*

*Keep Your Eyes Open*

Don't fool yourself thinking you can change someone or that what you see as faults aren't really that important. Once you decide to commit to someone, eventually their flaws, vulnerabilities, pet peeves and differences will become more obvious. If you love your mate and want the relationship to grow and evolve, you've got to learn how to close one eye and not let every little thing bother you.

You can't take someone to the altar to alter them.

You and your mate have many different expectations, emotional needs, values, dreams, weaknesses and strengths.

You are two unique individual children of God who have decided to share a life together. Neither one of you are perfect, but are you perfect for each other? Do you bring out the best in each other?

Do you compliment and compromise with each other, or do you compete, compare and control? What do you bring to the relationship? Do you bring past relationships, past hurt, past mistrust and past pain.

"Bad boys" often create inviting and intoxicating forms of drama—often perceived as playfulness, sexuality and fun. The magic of a connection with a man can be extremely powerful. You can get so caught up in the "high" of a new relationship that you lose your values, balance, self-control, spiritual salvation, identity, friends, family, health and even your job. Your reasoning and spiritual values may go out the door when an alluring bad boy walks in.

The dating habits of some bad boys are so predictable, they can be broken down into categories. Isn't it ironic that their behavior can be similar to some canine breeds. In the spirit of humor, I've drawn my own comparisons:

THE TOY POODLE—for show, everybody wants to pet him, is loving with others, he'll go to anybody who shows him attention.

THE HOUND—hunter by nature, instinctively likes to chase, very noisy and playful, not created for the domestic life.

THE TERRIER—feisty, persistent and aggressive, loyal companion, tries to dominate.

THE MASTIFF—bred to be strong and hearty, highly developed sense of property, ownership, very territorial and protective, independent, tends to be quiet and anti-social, he doesn't roam, he goes to work and comes straight home, trained to work hard, not wine and dine you with gifts and flowers.

THE RETRIEVER—requires a lot of daily exercise, unhappy kept indoors, gets bored easily, needs lots of attention, likes to play games.

*Characteristics of the Player/Bad Boy*

A "player" knows what to say and how to say it with charm to get what they want.

After you give a "player" what he wants, without consideration for your own needs, values and lifestyle, you are setting yourself up to be used and mistreated.

It is important that you maintain your self-respect and self-esteem. If you keep answering the phone and opening the door to your bedroom even though you are being mistreated, you are opening your heart and spirit to trouble, pain, more disrespect and abuse.

- Don't handle aggression with aggression.
- Always compliment good behavior.
- Understand that men are territorial.
- Don't be extra nice when the behavior is not warranted.
- Seek respect first. Love takes time.

We as women must not allow ourselves to be taken advantage of. Sometimes we can be our own worst enemy when we lie to ourselves about the state of our romantic relationships.

## Signs of Unhealthy Love

Ladies, don't get so caught up in the whirlwind romance that you ignore the signs.

Do you see any red flags waving that he is not the one?

Do you ignore these red flags:

- his lateness
- his rudeness
- his addictions
- those strange phone calls
- you loan him too much money
- his secretiveness

- ♦ you can never find him
- ♦ you don't spend holidays together
- ♦ you make excuses for his temper and abuse, possessiveness or mood swings
- ♦ the signs that he is immature, married, can't keep a job, unavailable
- ♦ "living down low" lifestyle

Disharmony in a relationship can cause frustration. It is best to be evenly yoked and of a common mindset with your partner. You should both practice open communication and be respectful of each other's feelings. Otherwise, you might find yourself experiencing these situations that cause stress.

1. Assuming your mate can read your mind eventually leads to resentment, withdrawal and anger. Communicate your needs, feelings and questions.
2. The mistake of getting into a relationship and neglecting your own pursuits and interests (education, travel, hobbies, values, self-esteem), friends and family.
3. You're only feeding the problem if you keep your door and body open to more temptation, confusion and pain. If you're not being treated right, you have the power, choice and spiritual authority to stop the madness.
4. Rushing into sexual intimacy, yielding more to your hormones than your heart, head or the Holy Spirit.

Settling for less because of peer pressure and feeling unworthy and inadequate because you are single.

5. Talking with too many people, bragging about the good or complaining about the bad in your relationship is not a healthy practice. Sometimes it's not always that bad and/or it's not always that good. Some people you talk with about your relationship problems either: a) really don't care; b) can't help you; c) would gladly take your place, and; d) gladly take your mate since you're talking about him/her so much.

6. Being too needy...expecting your mate to make you happy 24/7. Nobody has that responsibility but *you*. Or being too independent doesn't allow your mate to feel needed, included, appreciated or secure in the relationship.

7. Not compatible, communicating, cooperating and focused together on spending habits, savings and wealth building for future retirement and credit protection.

8. Thinking that when someone says they'll love you forever, it means forever. Their love may only be capable of a forever that is just for a weekend, a few months or a few years.

9. Don't be confused into thinking that kindness and small gestures of gifts equals romance or love.

10. Don't expect and believe that what your partner has done for another he will do for you, too.

11. Big mistake—Getting involved sexually, financially, emotionally or becoming parents without a commitment.

The Book of Isaiah 52 states: Awake, clothe yourself with strength, put on garments of splendor, shake off your dust and rise up, free yourself from the chains.

Are you one link in a chain of fools? Are you living with hopeless devotion, waiting and waiting in a one-sided relationship? Your head probably knows it doesn't make sense to keep trying, hoping, crying, waiting and wasting your time on someone who can't return your love. It's your heart that needs to see the truth. Your heart will keep remembering the good times and keep you in denial about the bad times.

Too many times during my counseling sessions with clients I see someone in pain and denial living only on hope and memories of what used to be. Even though their mate has told them they don't want to be in a committed relationship or they tell them that they are ready to move on with their life, that woman sitting in the chair in my office can't let him go.

Too many times women put their life on hold or they go into deep depression because they can't see beyond their pain, rejection and loneliness.

I believe that when someone tells you or shows you who they really are, believe it. Don't deceive yourself into thinking you can make someone love you or make someone stay or make someone change. Pick up the broken pieces and find yourself before you try to find someone new. Heal yourself and try to unload the emotional baggage before you carry into a new relationship.

*Signs of Healthy Love*

♥ You give each other room to grow, and you support each other's goals.

♥ You have separate interests, different friends, and meaningful relationships with friends and family.

♥ You feel secure in your own value and worth without the other person's validation.

♥ You trust your partner and are committed to each other and to the relationship.

♥ You willingly and lovingly compromise and negotiate any issues that may arise.

♥ You do not take ownership of each other's issues, or look toward your partner to fix your issues.

♥ You show support for your partner, yet you do not attempt to change, alter or force your opinions onto them.

♥ You enjoy their company, yet also are content with being alone.

♥ You communicate asking for what you need and want in your relationships.

♥ You seek to establish harmony, honesty, balance and teamwork.

♥ You realize change begins with yourself. You work on improving your self-esteem to avoid being used, extremely dependent or desperate.

♥ You learn the delicate balance of giving and receiving, serving and being served, nurturing and being nurtured, giving and receiving respect without jealousy, manipulation or deceit.

When stress or change happens in your life, your emotional habits will cause you to choose one of the following responses to **cope, endure, enjoy** or **excel** in your life:

- **Avoidance**  (resistance, fear, denial)
- **Anger**  (which creates more stress and resistance)
- **Allow**  it to continue (victimization)
- **Apathy**  (depression, procrastination)
- **Adapt**  (flexible, change, grow)
- **Acceptance**  (peace, let it go, go with the flow)
- **Action**  (faith, proactive courage)

Wake up and reclaim your power. Your words, thoughts, prayers and actions have influence.

You are in control of your destiny and responsible for your own happiness.

*Whateverso thy hand findeth to do, do it with thy might.*

—Ecclesiastes 9:10

Even when the path seems unclear,
I am empowered to do great things.
I trust myself to make decisions.
I believe that God lives in me and orders my steps.

*If you believe you are too blessed to be stressed, then*
*you know that it is a choice to rejoice. Faith, hope and*
*optimism are a choice.*

When things get tough,
I may be discouraged…
but never defeated.
I am determined to keep
growing and going.

*Love is patient, love is kind. It does not envy, it does not boast, it is not proud. It is not rude, it is not self-seeking, it is not easily angered, it keeps no records of wrongs.*

—1 Corinthians 13:1

# JOURNAL PAGE

_____

_____

_____

_____

_____

_____

_____

_____

_____

_____

# JOURNAL PAGE

_____

_____

_____

_____

_____

_____

_____

_____

_____

_____

# CHAPTER

4

## SPIRITUAL DISCERNMENT

*Women are "Going Through"*

There are so many women "going through." They have what Diana Ross sang about…"a sweet hangover."

When you have a love hangover your heart and hormones are telling you one thing and your mind and spirit are telling you something else.

You feel caught in a tug-of-war between your emotions and your good sense, between what you *want* to do and what you *should* do.

You feel lonely, angry, vulnerable and mad at yourself for ignoring the red lights that flashed and the flags that waved, warning you to stay away from Mr. Bad News.

I can remember a friend going through the relationship blues say, "How could I be so smart in one area of my life and yet so blind and weak in others? How could I have it so together in one part of my life and the rest of it is a mess?"

After the crying, honesty, praying, releasing and even some laughter, I've seen women realize that most of their anger is really directed toward themselves. They begin to see that they were leaving the door open for more drama and pain because of the little games they play just to stay connected in hopes that maybe…just maybe the relationship won't end.

I have also experienced my share of relationship blunders and blues. Some women can be smart with their money and foolish with their heart. And there are those who are smart with their heart and foolish with their money.

As women we can be smart in our career and weak in managing our home life. We can feel successful in our personal home life and feel like a failure at work. The list of contradictions and the tension of opposites goes on.

Once a woman realizes her worth and her role in the madness, the vicious cycle can stop.

♥ *A broken heart can be harder to heal than a broken bone. But it can begin to heal once…*

1. You see how you are allowing, promoting, creating or contributing to the problem because of your financial needs, insecurities, low self-esteem, denial, melancholy sentiments, romance addiction, pride, martyr syndrome, doormat syndrome or savior syndrome.
2. You accept the fact that you cannot change, rescue or make someone love you.

3. You stop compromising your sanity, health, spiritual values, finances, credit, joy, self-esteem, dreams and peace of mind.
4. Forgive yourself, throw away the pain and keep the lesson.
5. You have emotional boundaries drawing a line that allows NO craziness, abuse or temptation to cross.
6. You find safe harbors of friendships, counseling and spiritual support to heal your brokenness.
7. You sincerely pray for God's help to be free of the pain and old emotional patterns.

*If a Man Wants You*

If a man wants you, nothing can keep him away. If he doesn't want you, nothing can make him stay. Stop making excuses for a man and his behavior. Allow your intuition (or spirit) to save you from heartache.

♦ Stop trying to change yourself for a relationship that's not meant to be.
♦ Slower is better.
♦ Never live your life for a man before you find what makes you truly happy.
♦ If a relationship ends because the man was not treating you as you deserve then…"heck no," you can't "be friends."
♦ A friend wouldn't mistreat a friend. Don't settle. If you feel like he is stringing you along, then he probably is.

- Don't stay because you think "it will get better." You'll be mad at yourself a year later for staying when things are not better.
- The only person you can control in a relationship is you.
- Avoid men who've got a lot of children by many different women. He didn't marry them when he got them pregnant, why would he treat you any differently?
- Always have your own set of friends.
- Maintain boundaries in how a guy treats you. If something bothers you, speak up.
- Never, let a man know everything. He will use it against you later.
- You cannot change a man's behavior. Change comes from within.
- Don't *ever* make him feel he is more important than you are, even if he has more education or a better job than you. Do not make him into a quasi-god. He is a man, nothing more, nothing less.
- Never let a man define who you are.
- Never borrow someone else's man.
- If he cheated with you, he'll cheat on you.
- A man will only treat you the way you *allow* him to treat you.
- You should not be the one doing all the bending; compromise is a two-way street.
- You need time to heal between relationships.

Deal with your issues before pursuing a new relationship.

♦ You should never look for someone to *complete*
   you, a relationship consists of two *whole* individ-
   uals...seek someone complementary...not supple-
   mentary.

♦ Dating is fun...even if he doesn't turn out to be Mr.
   Right.

People don't value what they can have too easily,
whether they admit it or not. Let him miss you sometimes...when a man always knows where you are and
you're always readily available to him—he can learn to
take you for granted.

You are not a bad person because the one you love
doesn't love you in return. Read this message and other
materials to continue growing in wisdom, discernment,
self-esteem, faith, courage and love.

This book doesn't have all the answers but hopefully it
will give you some insights and food for thought.

It's time for the little girl who's seeking a man's approval
in order to experience love to grow up. It's time to stop
hoping that a man will become the man you want him
to be, when he shows you that he doesn't even have a
clue about what love is or how to be with a woman.

You are never going to meet someone who doesn't have
some issues or who isn't wounded.

The healthy behavior is to pay attention and take responsibility for your choices. Just because a man has sex

with you, it doesn't mean that he's spent even a second of his time deciding whether or not he wants to be with you in the future.

A man will *never* see you exactly the way you want him to see you, or value you exactly the way you know you should be valued, if...you're doing things just to seek and win his love and *approval*.

Men want to be challenged by the idea of meeting, attracting and pursuing a woman.

And then they want to win the woman over and feel stronger as a man for having done it.

The people who come into our lives are teachers. They enter our lives to help us grow. Unfortunately some of us in childhood did not get taught that life was full of lessons to be learned—instead we were taught that if something "bad" happens, it is because *we* are bad, *we* have done something wrong. We should not let these negative incidents stunt us. Instead, we should reflect, then grow positively.

I love myself.
I'm ready to bloom.
I am whole, blessed and
worthy of the success.

Instead of whining, wishing,
weeping, waiting, worrying
and feeling weary…
I will worship the Lord.
I will worship my way back
to wholeness.
God is good and so worthy
to be praised!

*What you may experience as rejection…could be God's gift of protection. Don't waste energy trying to make someone love you. You deserve more. You teach others how to treat you with the emotional boundaries you set…what you accept, reject and expect.*

Don't complain.
Life brings sunshine and rain.
Life can change without your permission.
Learn to be proactive, peaceful, patient,
positive, productive and prayerful.

♦ Life is too short to be mad and sad all the time. Take your happiness out of layaway.
♦ When you try to get even with someone, you are only letting that person continue to hurt you.
♦ Don't get even with those who have hurt you. Try to get even with those who have helped you in life.

*Trust in the Lord with all thine heart; and lean not unto thine own understanding.*

—Proverbs 3:5

# JOURNAL PAGE

_____

_____

_____

_____

_____

_____

_____

_____

_____

_____

# JOURNAL PAGE

_____

_____

_____

_____

_____

_____

_____

_____

_____

_____

# CHAPTER

## LEARNING TO LET GO

5

Has someone told you that you're crowding his space? Has the thrill gone but you're still trying to hold on?

I know it's hard letting go. But as you pick up the pieces of your self-esteem and pride you'll realize that being with someone who doesn't want to be with you is insane.

Give your heart some time to heal but listen to your head. You'll know when it's time to move on and move out. Pain happens in everyone's life, but misery is optional. You deserve to be loved and respected. Discover your voice and your value because you teach others how to treat you.

If you're recovering from a broken heart, there are things you can do to lessen the pain.

*Share Your Feelings*
Sharing your feelings with someone you trust may help you to feel better. That could mean simply talking with a friend or family member. For some, letting the tears flow seems to help them heal faster. For others, doing things

they normally enjoy, like seeing a movie or going to a concert, can be comforting. Talk with others who have gone through what you are going through. Find a support group in your area.

## Take Good Care of Yourself

A broken heart can be very stressful. But don't let the rest of your body get broken, too. Get lots of sleep, eat healthy foods and exercise regularly to minimize stress and depression and give your self-esteem a boost. When your heart is heavy with anger and sadness, it really can affect your heart physically. Be sure to get some form of exercise; take vitamin E; minimize consumption of fatty and fried foods; express and release your anger in a healthy way; enjoy nature; and laugh as much as possible. Humor is healing.

## Remember What's Good About You

Sometimes people with broken hearts start to blame themselves for what's happened. They may be really down on themselves, exaggerating their faults as though they did something to deserve the unhappiness they're experiencing. If you find this happening to you, stop it! Bad stuff happens to good people all the time. There are mysteries in life that you may never understand or deserve. Remind yourself of your good qualities, and if you can't think of them because your broken heart is clouding your view, get your friends to help you remember what's good about you.

*Keep Yourself Busy*

Sometimes this is difficult when you're coping with sadness and grief, but it really helps. This is a great time to redecorate your room, try a new hobby, go on a trip. Depression is sneaky, subtle and can consume you in darkness. Cancel your pity party and take back your power, joy, self-esteem and self-respect.

*Pray About It*

Ask the Lord to slap that bitter taste out of your mouth. Believe that the Lord can deliver you from the stress, pain, anger and depression. Pray believing and willing to see yourself as a whole, loving, capable and resilient woman. Pray for the discernment, discipline, wisdom and courage to begin your new season of life. Pray for everyone who is affected by your breakup, separation or divorce (i.e., children and other family members). Pray for the right words and right actions to keep your mind stayed on forgiveness, peace, love, grace, faith, joy and wisdom.

*Blessed is the man who does not walk in the counsel of the wicked or stand in the way of sinners or sit in the seat of muckers. But his delight is in the law of the Lord, and on His law he meditates day and night.*

—Psalms 1:1–2

I am excited about my future possibilities.
I reclaim my personal power to choose and
create the life I desire and deserve.
Sometimes I win and sometimes I learn.
I live in the now with gratitude
and let go of the past
as I learn the lessons they bring.

*I tell you the truth, if anyone says to this mountain,
"Go, throw yourself into the sea," and does not
doubt in his heart but believes that what he says will
happen, it will be done for him.*

—Mark 11:23

Every day I am finding my voice and value.
It is okay to be heard, seen and successful.
It's time for me to bloom!
I enjoy the process of working on my dreams and goals.
I'm keeping the main thing…The Main Thing!

*And you belong to Christ and Christ belongs to God.*
—1 Corinthians 3:23

# JOURNAL PAGE

_____

_____

_____

_____

_____

_____

_____

_____

_____

_____

# JOURNAL PAGE

_____

_____

_____

_____

_____

_____

_____

_____

_____

_____

# CHAPTER 6

## MAKE SMARTER LOVE CHOICES

*Start Today*

Teaching your heart to be smart is a process.

If you realize you have an unhealthy pattern of being in unfulfilling and toxic relationships or if your heart is broken into a million pieces, it's time to get clean and sober from the "love drug."

There are three stages of your process:

1. Numbed out, unaware of your pattern, no control.
2. Doing your best to be aware of the temptation, distraction, neediness and desperation, telling the truth to yourself, taking it one day at a time.
3. Aware of all your feelings, self-corrects, forgives yourself, finds other healthy and positive ways to fill the void, has boundaries, speaks up, recognizes that mistakes are your biggest teachers, demystifies yourself from the illusion while seeking help and the company

of others. As long as you feed into the fantasy, it gives you false hope, the false hope becomes a drug, it only feels good for a little while.

When you truly "want out" of the cycle, you will forgive yourself and move on stronger and wiser. You now begin to parent yourself and protect yourself from falling and being hurt. You now begin to stop believing, expecting or living a fairy-tale-fantasy-twisted-crazy drama, because you know only you can stop the madness and save yourself...the other person either can't or won't stop it for you. It's not the man, but the feeling you are missing. Once you find other healthy ways to fill the emotional hunger and emptiness, you will be happier.

Once you begin to let go of unrealistic expectations, see yourself as worthy and enough and learn to enjoy your own solitude, you will realize that you cannot give up the fantasy without struggle, you can't achieve any peace without effort. It will take time to begin to trust yourself, nurture yourself and heal the damage...but you *can do it!*

Tell yourself in the quiet times that you will start protecting yourself, loving yourself. Acknowledge and thank yourself for waking up and having the courage to do the right thing. Ask God for strength. Ask God to replace the hurt with some positive things to do and positive people to come into your life. Pray for the "willingness" to change because if you are not truly willing to let go, you will remain in bondage to a revolving door of misery. You've told it to your head...now you have to tell it to your heart.

- ♦ Believe that healthy love is possible.
- ♦ Be willing to assess your love life honestly.
- ♦ Connect the unhealthy aspects of your love life with your inner beliefs and past trauma.
- ♦ Change your beliefs to those that encourage healthy love.
- ♦ Let go of the fear of being alone or inadequate.
- ♦ Break any isolation patterns and connect with women who are healing and growing.
- ♦ Love yourself enough to ask the qualifying questions of a new love interest.
- ♦ Love yourself enough to say no to drama and yes to real love.
- ♦ Love yourself enough to heal the disease to please.
- ♦ Remember you cannot change someone.
- ♦ You can't rescue people from their misery.
- ♦ You can't expect someone else to make you happy.
- ♦ You can make a decision to end your misery. Change your number, close the door, don't return the phone call. Save yourself from drowning in your tears, get out of that funk, pack up the junk, stop singing those sad songs, wake up, turn on the light and move out of the house of blues. Reclaim your life!

Get motivated to follow your own dreams and do what you need to do to enjoy life. Ask the Lord to guide you to live in your gifts and higher purpose in life beyond relationships.

Like attracts like. The more you get yourself together… the more you increase your chances of attracting someone who has it together.

Most men don't spend so much time thinking about and getting depressed about relationships like we women. We've got to learn how to stop pouring all of our energy, passion and time into the wrong places.

Instead of just thinking about your dress size, your next date, where the shoe sale is or the next episode of your favorite television show…start thinking deeply, seriously, proactively, with serious determination, vision, persistence and faith…that you are growing and going to the next level in your life.

Make up your mind. Make a decision and the parachute will open. There is no change without pain. There is no gain without a positive train of thought. Don't be afraid of rejection, discomfort, fear and temporary setbacks. You could be moving even though you feel like you're standing still. Use your authority. Roll up your sleeves. Let the inner warrior woman in you shout, "Victory is mine!" Stand on the promises of God. Soar under the wings of other role models.

Sister…you may hate where you are now, but this is not your final destination, unless you give up and sit down. You must remain focused. The word of God says "no weapon formed against you shall prosper." So please understand this...weapons will be formed, they just won't prosper because God knows the plans He has for you. So you have to be strong (*spiritual, mental, financial, physical, emotional and in your relationships with others*) to fight against those things that will surely come to challenge a strong, focused and empowered woman like you. Let your iron be sharpened by the iron of other strong women. Don't let the enemy shut your mouth or distract you with issues of a faint and lonely heart or worry about what other people think.

Empower yourself. Don't waste and misplace your energy and passion into who is gonna love you or who is gonna like you. Direct your passion and energy toward your purpose, destiny and God-given talents and gifts. Create balance in your life. Read, pray, dream, journal, network, go to classes, ask questions, find a mentor, get a role model, listen to motivational and instructional CDs, turn on your brain, turn off the depression, cancel the pity party, stop sitting by the phone, take off your party shoes and put on your faith-walking shoes, let go of the drama-making people in your life, create new alliances, do something different, do something radical, speak differently, get rid of the clutter, write down your goals and dreams, make them specific and clear.

Right now I have the courage, energy and self-esteem to pursue my dreams and goals.

I can do this!

*The Lord is my rock, my fortress, and my deliverer, my God, my rock in whom I take refuge, my shield, and the horn of my salvation, my stronghold.*

—Psalms 18:2

I'm excited and inspired to begin taking actions
on my goals and dreams.

Something great is about to happen in my life.
I am ready, worthy and capable.

*Do you not know that the saints will judge the world?*
—1 Corinthians 6:2

# JOURNAL PAGE

_____

_____

_____

_____

_____

_____

_____

_____

_____

_____

# JOURNAL PAGE

_____

_____

_____

_____

_____

_____

_____

_____

_____

_____

# CHAPTER 7

## GET ON THE RIGHT TRACK

*Prescriptions From the Self-esteem Doctor*

♥ Get clean and sober from a love hangover one day at a time.

♥ Learn the qualifying questions to ask before commitment. It's so sad to see someone being pathetic and overeager. Desperation is a perfume that fills the room with negative energy. It's a sign of weakness and vulnerability instead of confidence and self-worth. Don't be an easy target for abuse, disrespect, heartache, financial loss and immature games from players and men who are unworthy of your heart.

♥ Speak up and protect the wounded girl, the queen and the child of God inside of you.

♥ Learn empowering affirmations to strengthen your self-esteem. Read the "affirmation for singles" often.

♥ Learn how to have "a life" in the meantime.

♥ Learn secrets to healthy relationships from reading and observing healthy role models.

♥ Break generational cycles of divorce, secrets, poor choices and stress, depression and emotional wounds from past and present relationships.

♥ Learn how to discern and distinguish the difference between what a bad and what an acceptable relationship feel and look like.

♥ Your emotional boundaries and tolerance level teach others how to treat you.

♥ Look in the mirror and see a queen. See a child of the most High God who deserves to be treated with respect, love, peace of mind, honesty and tenderness.

♥ Give yourself time. A heart can be slow to change. If you gave your all and you were caught in a web of deceit, your heart and soul may be black and blue. It takes time for sadness to go away. Keep the lesson but throw away your pain. Don't wish for someone to come back into your life who doesn't love and honor you. Don't be afraid of being alone. Trust God for your provision and healing.

Trust yourself that you will be able to get up again and move on with your life wiser, stronger, better and not bitter.

You are a precious gem in God's sight. You are a queen. Pick up your crown from the floor and know that you deserve more.

Almost everyone thinks they won't feel normal again, but the human spirit is amazing and the heart almost always heals after a while. Don't be discouraged. There are good men, husbands, fathers and friends in this world. There is hope. As you grow strong and wise, God will replace your ashes with beauty, restore your gladness and bless you with of love, joy and peace.

Everyone lives with some kind of disappointment, pain, struggle or sadness. Some choose to be bitter and some get better and rise above their circumstances. When life gives you lemons...make lemonade.

*So teach us to make the most of our time so that we may grow in wisdom.*

—Psalms 90:12

It's good to practice positive thinking, pray, prepare, plan and persistently pursue your dreams and goals. Enjoy the process of growing and achieving without becoming attached to the outcomes. Human nature seeks guarantees and predictability and avoidance of pain. Learn to adapt and accept uncertainty in life.

*But you, be strong and do not lose courage, for there is reward for your work.*

—II Chronicles 15:7

You attract into your life what you expect, what you prepare for, what you fear, what you give thanks for, what you believe, what you act upon, and what you think about all day.

*I do not hide your righteousness in my heart; I speak of your faithfulness and salvation. I do not conceal your love and your truth from the great assembly.*
—Psalms 40:10

What you eat, think and feel affects the quality of your health. Stress is an enemy of your state of mind and health. Negative and stressful people are more prone to heart disease. Learn how to respond to stress and changes in your life by being proactive, optimistic and prayerful. Until further notice…God is in control.

Are you living in a rut, doing the same thing and pondering the same thing day to day? Do you feel dull, powerless, tired, stressed, trapped and overwhelmed? This feeling is like being in a trance, a hypnotic state of numbness.

Sometimes it may seem like you're trapped in your pain and bad follows you wherever you go. Don't stop trying to make it better for yourself and your family. Stay focused on solutions and your sanity. Hold on to your spiritual rock of faith. Act as if your victory is already here.

Worship your way back into wholeness. Peace will come as you practice living in the now instead of visiting a past full of regrets, or living in anticipation of a future that hasn't arrived. Live gracefully with gratitude in the now.

In difficult moments, *seek* God.
In quiet moments, *worship* God.
In painful moments, *trust* God.
Every moment, *thank* God.

Failures are merely stepping stones to success.
Pain moves the heart to coping,
healing and the discovery of greater understanding
of myself and compassion for others.

*Therefore my beloved, be steadfast, immovable, always excelling in the work of the Lord...*
—1 Corinthians 15:58

I can express my individuality
without feeling selfish, strange or bad.
I am safe, blessed and divinely created.

*Bless the Lord, O my soul, and do not forget all his*
*benefits.*

—Psalms 103:2

# JOURNAL PAGE

_____

_____

_____

_____

_____

_____

_____

_____

_____

_____

_____

# JOURNAL PAGE

# CHAPTER

## 8

### THE MASKS WOMEN WEAR

For many years now I have been facilitating workshops and retreats helping women reduce emotional heaviness in their mind, heart and soul. Countless women have experienced emotional and spiritual healing, allowing them to enjoy success, peace and a healthy self-esteem.

Which mask do you wear? What emotional baggage have you carried too long? With God's grace, time, your willingness and courage to examine your life, you can erase the face of pain, shame, blame and low self-esteem.

The pain in your life has probably caused you to develop a set of survival skills to cope. These survival skills were necessary for the protection of your heart and soul. Wearing a mask can make you appear to be cold and disengaged. You could do this unconsciously for fear of being hurt or judged. You may learn to be guarded and watchful in your interactions with people so they don't get to know too much about you. The fear they could take advantage of you with that information is one reason. Or the reason could be your need to be accepted and approved of.

Many of us become skilled and creative in masking our pain. Over the years some accumulate layers of unhealthy coping skills to protect themselves, thus my term "emotional obesity," while others unconsciously gain physical weight to protect their physical body because they cannot cope with flirtation, sexual pressure, rape or other kinds of abuse.

Sisters, we run to the mall, the refrigerator or a secret lover. We cope by hiding in a bottle, hiding in our homes or the busyness of work. We cope with pain by working ourselves until we're bone tired or we pitch a tent in the valley of depression. We say yes when we should say no, to please other people. We can become needy or cold. We can sabotage our own blessings, remain stuck living in the illusion that someone owes us something or someone will rescue us to make us happy or save us from our misery.

My work with women on retreats, counseling and my own personal development have led me to believe that most women are haunted and depressed because they cannot find the answers to these questions:

+ Am I doing the right thing?
+ Am I making the right choice?
+ How long will my pain last?
+ Am I enough?
+ What is my purpose?

- Who is going to love me?
- How do I balance my career with my personal life?
- How can I choose me without being called selfish or feeling guilty?

If women never find the answers or learn to accept the process and patience required for an unfolding life, they will unconsciously learn how to wear a false mask to feel accepted, loved, powerful or safe.

This message promises to help you discover what emotional masks you wear and why you wear them.

We learn unconsciously how to navigate our way through the maze of family, work, church, social activities and peer pressure to survive and succeed. Unfortunately, however, some do it to scheme their way through life.

We wear many emotional and psychological masks:

1. PRETENSE mask: for show, to impress, to cover up shyness or feelings of inadequacy.
2. PRIDE mask: to hide our shame and embarrassment.
3. PAIN mask: fear and survival strategy because of past wounds and rejection.
4. PERFECTIONIST mask: to give the appearance that your life is in control and successful, your insecurities won't allow you to be authentic or exposed.
5. PROTECTION mask: you may appear cold, distant and withdrawn, you do this to avoid criticism, pity from others or scrutiny.

6. PLAYFULNESS mask: to avoid dealing with your pain, you play the clown, humor and silliness keep you from going to that dark place of pain.
7. PEOPLE PLEASER mask: you play the "nice" person to avoid rocking the boat, you would rather avoid conflict and confrontation, you seldom express your anger, needs or stress.
8. POWER mask: you live your life with the illusion of false control, you keep up an emotional wall.

When you put on a mask, you slip into another character and your external appearance is altered to fit the mood. But internally you're plagued by restless thoughts. Please don't be fooled by me. Don't be fooled by the face I wear, for I wear many masks that I'm afraid to take off and none of them are me. Pretending and hiding are an art of survival that is second nature to me, but don't be fooled.

I often give the impression I'm secure and that all is in control and great with me, that confidence is my name, coolness my game and I'm in command and that I need no one, but don't believe me, please don't believe me.

My face may seem secure but it is an ever-changing and concealing mask. Beneath lies my cry to belong, to connect, to be confident and to be acknowledged.

I panic at the thought of my weakness and I fear being exposed. Over the years I created a mask to hide behind nonchalant, sophisticated facades to help me pretend—to shield me from scrutiny. I learned to get by, hold back, become invisible and hide behind my own masks. Very few people get to see the real me.

I'm afraid that your glance and judgment will not be followed by love and acceptance. I'm afraid you'll think less of me and you'll laugh. I'm afraid that deep down, I'm nothing and that I'm just no good and that you'll see this and reject me. Sometimes I wear a mask of strength because I don't want to draw attention to myself. I don't want to be perceived as weak, needy and out of control.

On my job and even in my church, I often wear my masks of protection. I hide from the haters. I hide from the scrutiny of eyes that may see: my faults, my past, my weight/image issues, my mistakes, my insecurities, my financial lack, my fears, my family drama and dysfunction, my stuttering, my outer and inner scars.

So I play my game, my desperate pretending, with the facade of assurance without and a trembling child within. And so I created many faces to get through life.

I tell you everything is really okay. I don't really let you in. I say just enough to keep you from suspecting my insecurities.

Do not be fooled by what I'm saying. Please listen carefully and try to hear what I'm *not* saying—what I'd like to be able to say, but for survival I need to say, but what I can't say. I dislike hiding and suppressing my true self. I dislike the superficial masks I wear to just fit in or just not to be seen at all. I'd really like to be genuine, spontaneous and me, but you've got to help me. You've got to hold out your hand, even when it's the last thing I seem to want or need.

Even though I may seem distant, different, defensive or bold, you don't know what my life's story is...if it were told. We have all done different things to survive, to be loved and accepted. It's painful to be judged, denied and rejected.

You can help uncover my masks of feeling lost, invisible, unloved and unsure. You can help call me into aliveness each time you're kind, encouraging and gentle. Each time you try to understand me and show you really care, my heart opens and a mask is removed.

Who am I? I am someone you know very well. I am every man you meet and I am every woman you meet. If you choose to...you can encourage me to remove my mask. So do not pass me by. Speak to me. Don't harshly judge or dismiss me. Give me a chance to grow out of my cocoon and from behind my mask.

I am dying to the small self. I'm learning to put my ego, depression, fear and guilt on the shelf. I've been wrapped up in worry, hurry and strife. Where have I been all my life?

I'm coming out from behind my mask. I'm learning to love myself real fast. So many times I've given my power away to fear and what other people say. No longer scared, unfulfilled or a fake...my self-worth and confidence... now no one can take.

It does matter what I think, do, feel and say. I now know that I'm really okay. I'm removing the mask of fear.

I deserve success, happiness and love so dear. It's time to really be *me*...a strong and positive woman (man) you'll see.

How great it is to be alive in this universe. This life of mine I no longer curse. No time for self-doubt or feeling blue. I've got goals and dreams to pursue.

I am victorious, beautiful and free! I can rise and shine because love, faith, courage, strength and wisdom abide in me.

I'm coming from behind my mask living in truth and in the light at last!

When things get tough, I may be
discouraged…but never defeated.

I am determined to keep
growing and going.

*The gem cannot be polished without friction, nor man*
*perfected without trials.*

—Chinese proverb

Your life is a gift.
Open it.
Celebrate it.
Enjoy it.
Express it.
Share it.

Don't live an "unlived life."

*Let the morning bring me word of your unfailing love, for I have put my trust in you. Show me the way I should go, for to you I lift up my soul.*

—Psalms 143:8

# JOURNAL PAGE

_____

_____

_____

_____

_____

_____

_____

_____

_____

_____

# JOURNAL PAGE

_____

_____

_____

_____

_____

_____

_____

_____

_____

# CHAPTER
## WHO IS THE WOMAN EVE?

9

Eve learns to carry baggage and wear masks to hide or to seek love and acceptance. Eve can wear a mask to defend and protect herself.

Batman's character stated, "We all wear a mask." You can wear an invisible mask or create an invisible shield. People will approach you and try to get involved, but you zap them with your shield and they back away or turn and run. The shield is so subtle that at times you don't even know it exists, and you get confused by people who push away from you. This shield can take the form of coldness, wisecracking, fear of being hurt, aloofness, unwillingness to change or take a risk, fear of being taken advantage of, fear of intimacy, fear of failure, fear of hurting others, or other feelings that keeps you from connecting emotionally with another person.

Your self-esteem plays a big role in your life. It influences your thoughts, ideas and decisions. So many women suffer from what I call "emotional obesity." They live sluggish lives and suffer from the dis-*ease* of low self-esteem, depression, addictions, procrastination and may be living in abusive relationships. Your body naturally yearns to communicate. Your body will eventually want to express the feelings and emotions you've blocked. Emotions will eventually build up. I believe the excessive accumulation of shame, loneliness, regrets, anger, fear and grief create heavy layers of negative energy. Once the denial ends and willingness begins, the healing and letting go of accumulated layers and masks can occur.

> Negative emotions take a lot of energy to suppress and deny. It's like pushing a ball under the water.
>
> The ball of emotions will bounce back up sooner or later.
>
> Feelings are not buried dead; they are buried alive.

This chapter is my testimony, my therapy and my insights presented to you now as a gift and a weapon to deal with your inner demons. Only the enemy will be mad that you read this material.

Healing begins when you can identify your feelings.

Speak to your life situation with courage, love and authority. A great way to begin is by deepening your faith with gratitude, honesty, prayer, praise, worship and seeking God's wisdom.

Your strengthened faith lift will allow you to smile again. Honest recognition of your feelings and your defenses lift the veils that covered your true divine self. This is your time for a self-esteem makeover and a faith lift.

A spiritual and emotional healing allows everyone to see the real you. No fake. No hiding. No fear.

Just as Jesus called the twelve disciples and gave them authority and power to deal with all the demons and diseases in Luke 9:1, you have been given power and authority. The masks are no longer necessary as you learn to take back your power and joy. You can choose to deal with your inner demons. You can walk in authority, speak in the affirmative and take positive actions. Always remember your woman's worth, your power to choose and your power to heal.

Starting today you can lay hands on yourself. You can hug and affirm yourself. When you find yourself feeling stress, pain, temptation or fear, you can start observing your emotional patterns and coping skills.

- You will either suppress that "ball of confusion."
- You will find your voice and confess it.
- You will express your feelings and work through it in a healthy way.
- You will make some progress by growing in new positive coping skills.
- Or will you digress by going back to old behavior?

Whenever I facilitate the **12 Faces of Eve** retreat or seminar a common question is, "Can I be all of these faces? My answer is "yes." As I wrote the material and taught each session, I found myself in many of the faces. I think the characteristics and symptoms overlap. As you learn about the twelve common faces, you will discover parts of yourself in many.

You may discover that one is more dominant than the other. The key is to be open and truthful with yourself. The truth hurts, but more importantly...the truth heals.

# The Mirror is Talking

I'm learning how to be happy being me.
Imagine how happy and free I could be
If I took me...less seriously.

If I could laugh at my faults every once in a while
and accept my mistakes with a shrug and smile,
If I could take my setbacks and failures with stride
and remember my successes and blessings
with pleasure and pride,
Just imagine how happy I would be.

If I could become more loving, patient and wise
and not focus on others' opinions or my dress size,
Just imagine how content and free I could be.

If I stop procrastinating and take my dreams off the shelf,
If I thanked God more for His grace every time that I fell
and just run this race...what a testimony I could tell,
Just imagine how on fire I could be,
If I could look in the mirror and like what I see and stop
criticizing me.

I must confess if I could let go of the fear and stress and
I could live each day with courage, gratitude, faith and
love knowing my strength comes from within and
above.
Just imagine how peaceful I could be.

I like being me more and more each day.

As you read this message today.
I pray you are loving and accepting who you are
And if for some reason you're not
Maybe this is the moment that you will start!

Life is a journey—but sometimes it can feel like a long road trip. Be sure to travel with passengers going in the same direction. Along the road, you may experience a mixed bag of blessings, U-turns, potholes, changing scenery and many stops to refuel your tank. Be sure to keep your vehicle (body) in good shape and try not to look in the rearview mirror too much (your past). You can't afford to let people or circumstances drive you crazy. Instead, be driven to stay in peace instead of falling to pieces. Stay in your own lane of purpose, dreams and hopes. Carry your own map and allow the Lord to be your navigator.

Keep your eyes on the road—the best is yet to come.

*Wisdom is the principal thing; therefore get wisdom: and with all thy getting get understanding.*

—Proverbs 4:7

No matter how good or how right you are, the reality is that some people don't want to see you shine. You may have to work harder to prove yourself because of your gender, race, age, education, achievements, family/friends, talents, gifts, charisma, favor, social standing or your looks. It's not fair but it happens.

Once you have a deeper sense of self-esteem, self-worth and purpose, it can intimidate others...but it is also your strength. Jealousy is a cancer that is unfortunately in our families, workplace, church, school, and community. Hold your head up high. Don't give your power, joy, peace or destiny away to small-thinking people. Whether people are ignorant, prejudiced, insecure, malicious or jealous, you can't afford to allow them to contaminate your soul. Others are watching to see how you cope with darkness and the haters.

*Finally, brethren, whatever is true, whatever is honorable, whatever is right, whatever is pure, whatever is lovely, whatever is of good repute, if there is any excellence and if anything worthy of praise, let your mind dwell on these things.*

—Philippians 4:8

# JOURNAL PAGE

_____

_____

_____

_____

_____

_____

_____

_____

_____

# JOURNAL PAGE

# CHAPTER 10

## THE TWELVE FACES WE HIDE BEHIND

### SAD

Depression can come as your hormones change as a result of PMS or following a long period of sadness after experiencing the loss of: a loved one, your home, your marriage, your job, your youth, your car, money, etc.

Sadness can come from a hurt deep inside that crushes your heart and your spirit. Many times you cry, and the tears are hard to stop. You're not motivated to do the things you once looked forward to doing. Prolonged sadness can cause you to:

- feel anxious, "empty" or "numb"
- feel hopeless, like there's nothing to look forward to
- feel guilty or worthless
- feel lonely or unloved
- lose interest in regular activities—things are not fun anymore

+ have difficulty concentrating in school or on other activities, like reading or watching TV
+ sleep too much or not enough
+ not eat enough (smaller appetite) and lose weight or too much (bigger appetite) and gain weight
+ think about death—or sometimes attempt suicide
+ spend less time with friends and more time alone
+ cry frequently, often for no obvious reason
+ feel irritable (every little thing gets on your nerves)
+ feel restless (unable to sit still or relax)
+ have physical complaints, such as dry mouth, dry skin, difficult bowel movements, headaches, stomach or chest pain, vomiting, dizziness

*Sadness and grief from loss of a loved one*

Some things that happen to us never seem to make sense. I do pray that you keep your sanity and your faith during a time of grief after a loved one has passed. We get attached to our loved ones. We want them with us always. The word of God reminds us,

*None of us can hold back our spirit from departing. None of us has the power to prevent the day of our death. There is no escaping that obligation of that dark battle.*
—Ecclesiastes 8:8

Death comes into the room and leaves an awful silence. It's never welcomed or convenient. The time of grief is lonesome, stressful and awkward. You feel betrayed, confused and as if someone hit you in the stomach. You need great patience with your slow-healing heart. You can be angry one moment and sad the next. May the Lord show you His tender mercies, strength and peace in the days ahead. May He surround you with the love and comfort of family and friends.

## SHAME

Shame is a deep, debilitating emotion, with complex roots. Guilt, humiliation, demoralization, degradation and remorse are associated with shame. Webster's dictionary defines shame as "a painful emotion caused by consciousness of guilt, shortcoming, or impropriety." It is a painful feeling, and is very common among people suffering from: abuse, body-image issues, alcoholism, incest, rape, poverty, divorce, physical disability, addiction, abortion, family secrets, low income, imprisonment, AIDS, criminal record and racism.

Messages of shame can be rooted in culture, media, religion, family or your childhood past. As children we tend to blame ourselves for things that happen around us, because we are limited in our capacity to think about others being responsible.

A traumatized person no longer feels worthy of being loved, accepted and having good things happen to them in their life.

Feelings of shame and guilt will have you hide behind the mask of self-denial. Because it is less guilt-inducing to take care of others first, instead of yourself, you hide behind the mask of self-denial. You honestly believe it is better to serve others first, unaware that "guilt and shame" are the motivators for such "generous" behavior.

Shame is not the same as guilt. When we feel guilt, it's about something we did. When we feel shame, it's about who we are. When we feel guilty we need to learn that it's okay to make mistakes. When we feel shame we need to learn that it's okay to be who we are!

Overcoming shame will take some time. As you uncover this mask you will begin to hear yourself saying, "You know, I really *am* a good person!"

Maya Angelou's life story exemplifies overcoming trauma and shame. She said, "I can be changed by what happens to me, I refuse to be reduced by it."

If you can't forgive yourself, you are doomed to live in shame. When you can't forgive others, you live in blame. Holding grudges and wrapping yourself in the cloak of shame and blame can only block your blessings. Don't waste your power, time and energy on dead issues. Let go of the negative garbage in your life. Empty your mental trash can. Fill your heart, mind and soul with a winning attitude. Don't let the past rob you of your present or future. Peaceful and productive days will come as you make up your mind to focus on thinking, speaking and acting in a positive way. Always remember, prayer can't change the past but it can change your heart.

## STUCK

Do you feel trapped at home with the children or with no car? Have you run into a career wall at your job or in a dead-end or abusive relationship? Do you feel stuck living somewhere you don't want to be? Do you feel like you'll never finish your classes in order to graduate or get out of debt?

There are three stages of feeling stuck:

1. You feel stuck and don't know what it will take to help you feel a sense of relief, satisfaction or growth.
2. You feel stuck and you know what you want and need to get out of the circumstances...but you don't believe it can happen for you.
3. You feel stuck, you know what you want and need to get out of the circumstances...but you don't have the courage to take action.

How to get unstuck:

1. Weigh the pros and cons of taking action.
2. Learn to ignore your need for others' approval in order to take the most appropriate action for you.
3. Pursue the required actions despite the fear that it will create resistance from others, resulting in their efforts to make you feel guilty about taking such action.
4. Be open enough to determine if you are being too subjective, too emotional or sabotaging your own progress.
5. Be willing to accept honest, objective feedback about the ways you can change your behavior.

6. Make the effort to be less subjective, less defensive and more open in your search for truth, honesty, faith and sanity in resolving your problems.

7. Find something positive about your situation. If you focus on the things you hate about it, there is no energy left to focus on creating the changes you want.

8. If you're experiencing fatigue, mood swings, agitation, depression and your get up and go...just gets up and goes...these could be signs of a $B_{12}$ deficiency. Get up. Go to the health-food store. Get your supply of $B_{12}$ to energize yourself. You can't win in the game of life with poor health.

9. Feeling blue? Feeling down? Lift someone up today with an act of kindness. Take the attention off yourself.

10. Change is a part of life. Resentment, rebellion, resistance and regret only cause you more stress. You can't avoid change. You either become apathetic, angry, accept, adapt, or take action.

11. Whatever you are going through...stop to count your blessings.

12. Complaining, dishonesty, laziness and impatience only impede your success. If you're not properly managing or coping with the little things in life right now, you're not ready for the responsibility and rewards of the bigger things in life. *(Suggested reading*: Luke 16:10)

13. Let your self-talk affirm your strengths, faith, courage

and self-esteem. Tell yourself you can make it and that you can succeed in spite of it all.

Here's a great affirmation…

*I'm a diamond "growing" through some uncomfortable changes right now. This fiery process will burn away things, people, habits and beliefs I no longer need to hold on to. The polishing will make me shine with wisdom, faith, courage, peace and victory over my circumstances.*

*In spite of the pain from the cutting of the diamond within me, I will get better and not bitter because something great is about to happen in my life. I will stay in the Light…because I am precious in God's sight.*

*He who goes out weeping, carrying seed to sow, will return with songs of joy, carrying sheaves with him.*
                                                            —Psalms 126:6

Life can change without your permission. You could find yourself in the valley called "How did I get here?" or "How long will I be in this mess and stress?" or "Will I ever achieve my goals and dreams?" or the valley called "Broke, sick, tired, tied up and fed up." Been there, done that and said that. I agree with Oprah Winfrey's state-ment: *"Doing the best at this moment puts you in the best place for the next moment."*

Don't allow this fast age of microwave food, e-mail, overnight express and digital film development to set you up to think you can also resolve your life issues that fast.

When you are in the *season of waiting* and in between where you used to be and where you want to go, don't give up. You can choose to go through the seasons in your life resisting and angry. Or you can *grow through* the seasons in your life.

Life brings us valleys and mountaintop experiences. Learning how to be strong, focused and resilient is so key to your success and sanity. Liberation from a dead-end job, an addiction, financial bondage or liberation from an oppressive society takes planning, time, action, patience and faith.

Nelson Mandela teaches, "There is no easy walk to freedom anywhere, and many of us will have to pass through the valley of the shadow of death again and again before we reach the mountaintop of our desires."

*Now we see but a poor reflection as in a mirror; then we shall see face to face. Now I know in part; then I shall know fully, even as I am fully known.*
                              —1 Corinthians 13:12

Are you waiting for the perfect conditions or a guarantee before you take action?

Whether you want to write a book, buy a home, start your own business, leave a dead-end job or leave an abusive relationship, it takes decisive action.

Don't get stuck in the paralysis of analysis. Dr. Martin Luther King Jr. stated, "Faith is taking the first step even when you don't see the whole staircase."

With action and faith anything is possible. Without them, you're just dreaming.

*So teach us to make the most of our time so that we may grow in wisdom.*

—Psalms 90:12

**SINGLE**

Are you living single or single again after a relationship ends? Feelings of inadequacy, insecurity, fear, anger and unworthiness are those "emotional calories" that can cause emotional obesity.

An unfortunate breakup or divorce doesn't doom you to a life of loneliness. Sometimes, newly widowed or divorced people unwittingly select the "wrong" partners after a loss.

The woman soon discovers that she either made a mistake or that the courtship that suited the couple's needs at a very vulnerable time is just not suitable for the long term. When they reflect back, many people can see some positive effects from their interim "dating"; it helped them make the transition to widowhood or post-divorce a little easier; it helped build their self-esteem; it made them feel that they could be attractive and desirable, etc.

Please think about this— When your body is hungry, you feed it. If you value your health you don't give it junk food. You take the time to prepare a delicious and healthy meal. If you don't want to be sick, you won't ingest something that is harmful to your body. But sometimes when you are really hungry, you tend to eat whatever is available. Under those circumstances, you may eat whatever is available and discover later that you are still hungry.

This same scenario happens when your soul and heart are hungry. If it's been a long time since you've had a healthy relationship, you may settle just being with whoever is available. You may compromise your health, peace of mind, financial stability, spiritual values and integrity if you're really "hungry." If you're naive, desperate or lonely, you may not be too selective about who to date.

A mind set of desperation relates to the health of your self-esteem. As your self-esteem grows strong you can avoid the "I" factor to boost your Relationships IQ.

The "I" factor comes into play when you find yourself entangled in an emotionally draining relationship. When a woman's fear of being alone keeps her in an abusive or adulterous relationship, she needs to understand the "I" factor. A woman with a wounded self-esteem can easily be seduced by the flirtation, temptation and the sense of belonging (even though it's part-time and secretive) with online relationships. A man who does not respect you and senses that you have your guard down knows that your desperation gives him liberty.

The following components make up the "I" factor:

Insult—When your self-esteem is healthy, your mind, heart, and spirit would recognize when you are being insulted. Relationships that are disrepectful will only dishonor your soul and shatter your spirit. You are worth more. Don't allow your desperation to say "yes" to someone who only insults and humiliates your very existence. You deserve much better.

Injury—Creeping around in relationships that are secretive, adulterous, or abusive hurts not only you, but hurts and injures those who care about you. You're not in this world alone. Every choice you make affects those connected to you.

Illusions—After falling in love, you can fall out of reality. Real love grows beyond the illusions, romantic myths, expectations, and weekend getaways. Real relationships experience everything from boredom to ecstasy, joy and pain, sickness and health, compliments and criticism, devotion and disappointments. Don't allow illusions and unrealistic expectations to distort your thinking and behavior.

Just because no one has been fortunate enough to realize what a diamond you are, doesn't mean you shine any less.

Just because no one has been smart enough to figure out that you can't be topped, doesn't stop you from being the best.

Just because no one has come along to share your life, doesn't mean that day isn't coming.

Just because no one has made this race worthwhile, doesn't give you permission to stop running.

Just because no one has realized how much of an awesome woman you are, doesn't mean they can affect your femininity.

Just because no one has come to take the loneliness away, doesn't mean you have to settle for a lower quality.

Just because no one has shown up who can love you on your level, doesn't mean you have to sink to theirs.

Just because you deserve the very best there is, doesn't mean that life is always fair.

Just because God is still preparing your king, doesn't mean that you're not already a queen.

Just because your situation doesn't seem to be progressing right now, keep believing, keep hoping, keep praying.

*Keep being exactly what you are already...COMPLETE!*
*Keep on doing what you do best...BEING A WOMAN*
*OF GOD.*

—Author Unknown

## SELF-ESTEEM

Are you wearing a mask because your self-esteem is low? Are you shy? Do you suffer from the disease to please, feel insecure or invisible because of your appearance, socioeconomic status, soul wounds from abuse, etc.

What increases your self-esteem:

♦ having a sense of belonging to God and a family
♦ achievement; when you do well, you feel well
♦ living independently; the ability to be resourceful and take care of your needs
♦ enjoying some form of creative expression
♦ having personal values and boundaries
♦ positive self-talk instead of putting yourself down

What diminishes your self-esteem:

♦ taking no action
♦ neglect
♦ being in denial
♦ indecision
♦ making excuses

♦ wrong associations
♦ compromising your values
♦ suffering in silence
♦ indifference
♦ tolerating disrespect
♦ overdependence on the approval of others
♦ playing the blame game

Find your voice and develop the courage, faith and self-esteem to reclaim your power and peace of mind. There are many different battles to fight. You need a strong sense of self-esteem, self-worth and self-respect to deal with:

♦ your supervisor and coworkers
♦ customers/public service
♦ institutional racism
♦ family or friends taking your kindness for weakness
♦ job promotion
♦ your child in the system
♦ custody/child support
♦ parent guilt
♦ healing the shame
♦ poor customer service
♦ bill collectors
♦ civil rights abuses
♦ domestic violence
♦ an unfaithful mate
♦ competing in sports, sales, interviews, etc.

Value your heart, body, time, talent, uniqueness and skills.
Speak up and find your voice.

People learn how to treat you based on how you value yourself.

## STRESSED/SCARED

Are you feeling alone, afraid of change, afraid of financial struggle or illness? Are you afraid to defend yourself, afraid to ask for what you want or afraid to follow your heart?

Do you hear yourself saying: *"I keep telling myself that this is something I just need to get through. I still feel so pathetic for allowing fear to control me. Why can't I just snap back?"*

Stress usually happens as you experience change, conflict, frustration or pressure. If you can't cope with stress, it will drain your vitality, faith and positive coping skills. Trying to keep up and stay up can cripple you emotionally and spiritually. God's word teaches us to "be joyful always; pray continually; and give thanks in all circumstances." (I Thessalonians 5:16–18)

> *Serenity is not the absence of problems,*
> *but the ability to cope with them.*

What are you avoiding? Are you afraid of taking a risk because of a past experience?

Fear is a faith killer. Fear robs you of peace of mind. Fear is a liar. Fear blocks your blessings and growth. Procrastination is a by-product of fear. Don't wait until you think you have all the answers and courage to get started. Those things will come as you begin to take those small steps.

Once you make UP your mind and get UP and moving, the favor, mercy, grace and blessings of God begin to move on your behalf.

You say: "I'm afraid."
God says: *I have not given you a spirit of fear.*
 (II Timothy 1:7)
You say: "I can't do it."
God says: *You can do all things in Me.* (Philippians 4:13)
You say: "I'm always worried and frustrated."
God says: *Cast all your cares on Me.* (I Peter 5:7)
You say: "I don't have enough faith."
God says: *I've given everyone a measure of faith.*
 (Romans 12:3)
You say: "I'm not smart enough."
God says: *I give you wisdom.* (I Corinthians 1:30)

**SURVIVOR**

Most people look at you and don't see your emotional scars. Maybe they don't know that you have survived: abuse, violence, loss of a home, layoff, illness, surgery, financial setback, divorce, addictions. Maybe you have buried your child, husband, father or mother.

It takes strength to feel a friend's pain
   **It takes courage to feel your own pain.**
It takes strength to hide your own pain
   **It takes courage to show it.**
It takes strength to endure abuse
   **It takes courage to stop it.**
It takes strength to stand alone
   **It takes courage to lean on another.**
It takes strength to survive
   **It takes courage to live again.**

Survivors know about endurance, faith and courage. They have tasted their own tears. Compassion, wisdom and strength were gifts from their pain. They turn their pain into poetry, healing ministries, books, creativity and a life of testimony. My warning for the survivor is to be careful not to let your heart become hard and bitter. Don't wear the mask of *"I don't need anything and I don't need anybody."*

## SILENT SUFFERER

Your pride wants you to hide your feelings and needs. You don't allow others to help you. You don't want to be a burden or embarrassed because of your circumstances. You carry your sadness and anger inside. You can be moody, passive, argumentative or a martyr. You live with silent screams or secrets.

Some women are not divorced, but they have emotionally left the marriage. Some women show up for work, but they are absent in enthusiasm, commitment and a sense of duty.

Some women are still alive and breathing, but they are dead in spirit because they have been discouraged, their hearts have been broken, they had a song beat out of them, swallowed other people's bitterness and lost hope.

When you learn to let go and open up, you will lose the emotional obesity from carrying so much stuff. You can't do it alone. It's not healthy to keep holding in your needs, fears, anger and pain.

## SELF-ABUSE

Addictions, neglect and tolerating or imposing pain on yourself are symptoms of self-abuse. If you feel unworthy, inadequate, hopeless or angry, you may hurt yourself instead of expressing your rage.

What do hurt people do?

1. Hurt themselves
2. Hurt someone else
3. Or look for love in twisted and unhealthy ways

There's a sad trend of self-mutilation among young girls. Self-injury transcends gender, age, religion, educational and income level. It may be accompanied by a range of psychiatric problems such as depression or other mood disorders, obsessive-compulsive disorder, addictions, eating disorders or psychotic disorders. Self-abuse can be as mild as neglecting your daily self-care and harsh self-criticism, or as extreme as thoughts of suicide. As you grow in self-appreciation, you will begin to take better care of yourself. You will establish boundaries so that nothing or no one that means you harm can hurt you. You will speak up. You will get up and go to: the doctor, your work, class, church, rehab, the movies, dancing, your hairstylist, see family and friends, etc.

Please seek professional help if you recognize your self-abuse is out of control.

## SUPERWOMAN

A superwoman is usually the: oldest child, an over-achiever, workaholic, serving on too many committees, foster mother, college student, dutiful daughter, working wife/mother, the caregiver for an aging parent or physically challenged child. She has not learned how to say no or delegate duties. She is stretched to the limit. She doesn't go to bed at the end of the day...she passes out from exhaustion.

Female family members (wives, grandmothers, daughters and sisters) are the primary caregivers for millions of terminally ill patients. They often serve as the sole providers of an array of nursing, homemaking, transportation and personal-care needs. She is *over responsible*, striving to make life "right." She will overgive of herself and be willing to do anything in an attempt to make everyone happy. You may be multitasking or living on the fast track. Something's got to give before you experience burnout.

**MEMO TO THE SUPERWOMAN:**

*Worry, exhaustion and stress only rob you of your blessings and the energy you need to fulfill your divine destiny. Trust Me and cast all your cares on Me. I have seen how you keep going and giving. I have seen you endure some tough times and achieve some goals. Take care of yourself. Take off your superwoman cape. Delegate some tasks. It's OKAY to say no without feeling guilty. Do not feel personally and totally responsible for everything and everyone. That's MY job."*

*Love,*
*God*

## STOVE

The *stove woman* in the family is my metaphor for "Big Momma." The *stove woman* in the family or office is the one everyone goes to for: help, money, support, ideas, bail money, school money, babysitting, plan the reunion, plan the holiday dinners, etc. She is the glue that keeps the family together, the church together, the choir together, etc. Nothing is cooking unless the STOVE is on. Eventually the stove gets burned out.

The *stove woman* becomes an emotional sponge. She soaks up all the negative energy around her from the drama and stress in the family, church or workplace. Her emotional body is heavy and she becomes sluggish, sick and stressed.

The *stove woman* usually wears the mask of "What do you need? I'm all right. I don't mind. I don't need anything. It doesn't matter."

The *stove woman* subconsciously believes...

I must be nice to people no matter how they treat me.

Everyone needs me and they would be lost without me.

I am depended upon. It is my role to keep everything together, no matter what price I have to pay.

This is the way things are supposed to be.

I can never win in the situation I am in, but I can't leave it.

She needs to know that she doesn't have to buy love. She needs to learn how to say no without feeling guilty. She needs to find ways to take care of herself before giving herself away until there is nothing left to give but resentment.

## SANE & SAVED

You have discovered a balanced and blessed life. You have a relationship with the Lord. You no longer give your power away to people or circumstances. You cope with adversity. Your faith is renewed. Your heart is healed. You claim your voice, your value and the victory over the enemy. You walk in your divine purpose. You have established emotional boundaries. You can say no to demands and requests without feeling guilty. Your prayer life keeps you strong in spite of life's difficulties. You take time for prayer and self-care.

Rather than reacting based on past fears and experiences, you stay in peace rather than falling to pieces when change, stress or conflict arise.

You have an ability to enjoy each moment as you practice living the "now moment."

You lose interest in judging yourself and judging other people.

After experiencing pain, loss and setbacks, you grow in acceptance and renewal instead of having a pity party.

You don't worry so much anymore. You tell yourself, "I'm too blessed to be stressed."

You don't spend a lot of energy trying to control others or fix other people's problems.

You have frequent overwhelming episodes of appreciation.

You have frequent outbursts of smiling and praising God.

You have an ability to let go and not sweat the small stuff.

Your math is improving because you are counting your blessings more and more. It spite of circumstances…you count it all joy.

Your heart is more open to receiving and giving love.

You have more conversations and communion with God, your ever-present source of provision, peace and prosperity.

You will demand less and less that events and people conform to your insistent cravings. This indicates a falling away of a false belief of control, because you are maturing emotionally and spiritually with contentment.

Accepting personal responsibility includes:

♦ Acknowledging that you are solely responsible for the choices in your life.

♦ Taking an honest inventory of your strengths, abilities, talents, virtues and positive points.

♦ Accepting that you cannot blame others for the choices you have made.

♦ Tearing down the mask of defense or rationale for why others are responsible for who you are, what has happened to you and who you are becoming.

♦ Recognizing that you are your own best cheerleader. It is not reasonable or healthy for you to depend on others to make you feel better about yourself.

♦ Letting go of your sense of responsibility for others. You are protecting and nurturing your spiritual and emotional well-being.

♦ Taking preventive healthy steps of structuring your life with time management, stress management, confronting fears and burnout prevention.

♦ Working out anger, hostility, pessimism and depression over past hurts, pains, abuse, mistreatment and misdirection.

♦ Inner-gizing your *spiritual self* which generates faith, integrity, inner peace, courage and compassion.

**How?** Meditation, prayer, trusting God for your needs, inviting the Lord into your life to fix the broken places and strengthen your discipline, cultivating obedience and trust, finding a good spiritual church home, praise and thanksgiving, forgiveness, fasting, getting outside, enjoying nature, providing service to others, reading and study, surrender, silence, solitude, spiritual retreat.

♦ Inner-gizing your *emotional self* generates creativity, self-esteem and confidence.

**How?** Developing a sense of humor, enjoying your hobbies, creativity and special interests, speaking up and protecting your emotional boundaries and rights, being honest in communicating your feelings, writing in your journal, enjoying loving supportive relationships with family, friends, healing the past, forgiving yourself, forgiving others, taking a vacation or retreat, balancing work with some time for leisure.

♦ Inner-gizing your *mental self* generates enthusiasm, ideas and intelligence.

**How?** Reading, problem solving, doing puzzles, playing chess, concentrating on a task, deep breathing, going on a fast, writing/planning your goals, having a career that challenges and stimulates your mind, watching less TV, taking a nap, taking a vacation.

♦ Inner-gizing your *physical self* generates energy, stamina and good health.

**How?** Exercising, deep breathing, stretching, walking, drinking sufficient water, eating healthy foods, eliminating toxic substances (cigarettes, caffeine, alcohol, drugs), taking daily herbal/vitamin supplements, fasting, reducing stress and negative thinking, good ventilation, sunlight, going dancing, enjoying nature, having proper rest, pampering your body with a massage, manicure, facial, pedicure, steam bath, taking a nap, taking a vacation or retreat.

The larger the waistline...the shorter the lifeline. Most Americans eat too much fast, fried, frozen and fatty foods. It is not how long you live, but how you feel while you're living.

*Beloved, I pray that you may prosper in all things and be in health just as your soul prospers.*

—3 John 1:2

Be optimistic. Anticipate the best possible outcome. The word optimism is derived from the Latin ops, meaning power.

You create your own feelings and make your own decisions. People and events do not cause feelings, but they can trigger your mental habits.

Hope is essential to a vital life. Your happiness or your misery depends upon what you tell yourself, how you treat yourself and how you interpret your world.

Do you believe what you see or do you SEE what you believe? Train your brain to focus on your options and optimism instead of on your obstacles.

Optimists have faith and see beyond their present circumstances. The times when optimism really pays off occur when you are faced with a life problem, challenge or setback. Being optimistic at these times will increase your resilience, help you maintain hope and improve your chances of a successful or acceptable outcome.

*If ye have faith as a grain of mustard seed, ye shall say unto this mountain, remove hence to yonder place; and it shall remove; and nothing shall be impossible unto you.*

—Matthew 17:20

Life does not offer straight lines.
Life is full of curves, turns, ups and downs.
Whether somebody is sharing the ride with you
or you are going it alone...enjoy the ride.

If you're enjoying it but someone behind you is
screaming with fear, don't let their fear steal your joy.

If you're down now...hold on, you'll be up again soon.

*The Lord works righteousness and justice for all oppressed.*

—Psalms 103:6

# JOURNAL PAGE

_____

_____

_____

_____

_____

_____

_____

_____

_____

_____

# JOURNAL PAGE

_____

_____

_____

_____

_____

_____

_____

_____

_____

_____

# CHAPTER
11
EMOTIONAL PATHWAY FOR PERSONAL
AND SPIRITUAL GROWTH

I'm so excited to share these empowering messages to help you uncover your mask and discover your power and beauty. I know that the right information can lead to transformation. Knowledge is power when it is applied.

Sometimes before we can get on the road to a positive relationship, we have to overcome hurdles. These roadblocks can make us feel abandoned and useless. But it can be as easy as seeking out information, then putting one foot in front of the other to begin the journey.

Recognize where you are now in this pathway of emotional healing. You will experience your breakthroughs and gain momentum to have a more abundant life.

Don't remain frozen in frustration and isolation. Read all these pages often. Connect with women's healing circles and ministries like mine, or one near you. As the fire sharpens the iron, you will experience your life growing to a new level of awareness, clarity, strength and joy.

I've discovered not all men, but most men, mask their pain by walking around with a chip on their shoulder, talking loud, escaping into sports, violence, sex or work. Their pain is usually externalized. The opposite is true for so many women. Our pain is internalized. We become emotionally obese as we swallow the "emotional calories" because we don't want to appear mean, selfish or unChristian.

One of my favorite self-esteem quotations is from the movie *Joy Luck Club*. This was a story about mother-and-daughter relationships and a woman's worth. In the film, the young daughter's mother committed suicide as a result of shame. The daughter stood at her mother's casket, saying, "That is the day I learned to shout." She found her voice. She reclaimed her authority and heritage after family members tried to suppress her, deny her and shame her and her mother.

My sibling sisters and I were taught by our parents to be *ladylike*, timid, seen and not heard. I don't ever remembering expressing anger or disagreement as a child or in the early years of my marriage. I learned to be the dutiful daughter that never rocked the boat. So you can imagine the leaps of learning I've had to make. Learning to find my voice has been an interesting, long and healing journey. As an adult, I was slow in learning my own voice and value. My anger issues eventually came up.

Unmet needs and unspoken feelings become layers of

unfelt pain. As these layers build up we become emotionally obese. We learn to lie about or hide our feelings. We either hurt ourselves or we hurt others.

In the past I looked for love in the wrong places. Over the years I had a couple of outbursts at peculiar and unexpected times. I was either: burning the dinner, crying, yelling, driving away fast or cursing. This was so out of character for me. Some can call it PMS. But I know now it was unexpressed and suppressed anger coming out at the wrong time to the wrong person. To God, be the glory! His mercy and grace have saved me from some destructive and unhealthy coping habits.

Ladies, we are leaders, lovers, lifters and load carriers. We call ourselves everywoman, diva, queen, prayer warrior, CEO, superwoman, Ma'dear, head of the household, student, senior citizen, sexy, tired, entrepreneur, prosperous, believers, breadwinners and beautiful.

Perhaps you're reading this material because you realize it's time for a makeover. Maybe you realize that you are living your life out of control, out of order or just plain out of energy, faith and self-esteem. I can only write this book because I have seen days when I felt like I was only being held together by some scotch tape and a prayer. I've seen days when I have questioned my sanity, my faith, my purpose, my marriage, my parenting skills, my decisions and my self-esteem.

Writing these messages *and* sharing these insights in my **12 Faces of Eve** seminars in the past couple of years allowed me to heal. I discovered the masks I was wearing to protect myself, survive and negotiate relationships. I discovered the sacred unspoken contracts I made unconsciously to keep the peace, to please others or even to avoid success because of guilt.

While teaching these seminars I was helping others. But in return I gained deeper clarity and understanding about my own issues.

I continue to empty my mental and emotional trash can of guilt from poor choices, lost time, the dis-*ease* to please and a wounded self-esteem.

Have you given your power away to other people? Are you suffering with emotional scars, shame, secrets and silent screams? Do you hear the voice of your inner critic putting you down?

Some of us were told that we were too bossy, arrogant, too loud, too ambitious, too pretty, too dark, too light or just "too much." Some of us were told to lower our standards, tolerate the intolerable or just fit in where you could get in. Some of us had our dreams kicked out of us. Some of us were told to get out of that mirror and some of us were never affirmed about our inner and outer beauty. And yes, some of us have been waiting for someone to rescue us. Some of us have been derailed from our goals because of divorce, illness, grief, depression, debt, diapers, deadbeat friends and/or mates.

When you have been told you are no good or when you have felt invisible, incompetent and insignificant, it is like being hypnotized and put under a spell. Once you wake up and snap out of the trance, you begin to realize the truth about your divine, significant, whole, loving and capable self. You will begin to remove the disguises and accept no more compromises. You can learn to break the trance of low self-esteem and fear.

An African proverb teaches, "Around every flower are insects." When you decide to show the world your beauty, uniqueness and place in the garden of life, the insects will try to discourage you. The insects are those who criticize you and try to keep you from growing in the sunlight.

My life's work is dedicated to watering flowers like you. If people are not nourished in a good garden, they never fully bloom into their greatness. They end up with unfulfilled dreams, untapped talent and trapped in depression, addicted to unhappiness or even lost in the criminal system.

Without self-esteem, human and civil rights can be violated. The cycle of living with debt, divorce, depression, abuse, addictions and oppression continues to pass from one generation to the next.

Unfortunately, too many experience soul wounds and emotional or physical violence that damage self-esteem.

You are a flower that can be crushed by abusive partners, parents, friends, a negative social atmosphere and even employers.

Give yourself permission to make time for yourself. Where do *you* fit in on your list of things to do? Do you make time for relaxation, pampering, hobbies, reading, journaling, praying, solitude?

God created women as nurturers, sensitive and compassionate to others. We are natural caregivers. Somehow, too many women have never learned how to take care of themselves. Society and cultural values have taught women to seek their validation, identity and happiness outside of themselves. Women have become silent sufferers in the name of sacrifice, altruism and being a nurturing superwoman.

You can learn to be a steel magnolia...strong yet tender.

You can rise again after your individuality, spirit and personal power have been crushed. Self-esteem wellness strengthens your confidence to make decisions. It empowers you to respond effectively in situations where people may take advantage of you.

As you grow to have a clear and positive sense of self-worth, you will communicate to others what you want and need. Feeling secure with your personal boundaries, beliefs and behavior, you can "give and take" in an appropriate way without compromising your values. You are true to yourself because you don't need another person's approval to feel good about yourself. Approval is nice, but your sense of being a good person does not depend on it.

Emotional wounds from your childhood, divorce, illness, racism and unhealthy media messages can leave deep self-esteem scars. There are many women, like me, who grew up on childhood fantasies. Stories of the damsel in distress unconsciously shaped our expectations and self-worth. Storybook character Rapunzel was powerlessly trapped in a tower until a man saved her. Cinderella was trapped as a slave in her family, until a prince saved her. Snow White was cast into a deep sleep until she was kissed by a prince. And let us not forget Dorothy, lost and desperately seeking the Wizard. He was a fake and told her she had the power all the time. The story ended with Dorothy waking up from a nightmare.

Women suffering because of abandonment, rejection, abuse or failure often compromise their values to win approval from others. They either isolate themselves, do things that are unsafe and violate their own sense of what's right or they overcompensate by doing things in excess. The woman who feels left out or left behind often asks, *What did I do wrong? Where will I find love for me?* Her sense of guilt, shame and pain is so overwhelming that these questions haunt and torment her.

There are better questions to ask yourself to unlock the psychological locks in your mind. Victimized no more, your spirit begins to soar. You begin to see yourself as divinity in motion, no longer emotionally crippled.

The healthy questions to ask on the road to recover-

ing self-esteem are: *What can I learn from this experience? What can I do to heal myself? What is my
habitual pattern of escape and avoidance? What are my
false comforts? How can I take care of myself without
seeking approval from others? What keeps me from
loving myself? What keeps me from forgiving myself?
What keeps me from giving myself permission to be
happy? Why do I feel like I don't belong? Who told me
I am selfish, no good or ugly? Why do I feel unworthy
of love and success?*

As you learn to value your peace of mind, self-respect
and wellness, you will make wiser choices to decrease the
stress, anger, sadness and sense of victimization.

Building healthy self-esteem is *not* about self-absorption
or denying the salvation power of God in your life.

Please *do not confuse* building self-esteem with promoting egotism, arrogance, conceit, narcissism or a sense of
superiority.

This message is a tool to help you find your voice,
create positive self-talk and develop self-competence.

Self-esteem has psychological, sociological and spiritual
dimensions. The foundation for your self-esteem was
shaped while you were a child. Your home was your first
garden. Did you receive a lot of watering?

Self-esteem can be damaged by lack of nurturing from
family or later in life from trauma, setbacks, illness,

divorce, abuse, racism, distorted media messages and much more.

Self-esteem is more than just self-love. It's a deep sense of self-worth based on the mastery of specific traits, skills, attitudes and positive feedback from others. Self-esteem is the practice of living with self-acceptance, self-responsibility, self-assertiveness and integrity.

You esteem yourself when you respect, honor and love your life (*heart, mind, body, soul, choices, past, present and future possibilities*). Your life is a gift. Your unique talents and individuality are a gift.

Self-esteem comes from awareness of your spiritual heritage. Beyond the dysfunction, divorce or disappointments from your biological parents, your heavenly Father loves you. You are an heir to the Kingdom. This awareness helps you stand taller as you esteem your life and your worthiness. God's love for you is the redeeming deliverance power that can salvage any broken pieces of your heart and soul.

In talking and praying with so many as I worked through my own issues and their issues, I discovered many things. For example, we don't want to feel the pain of past hurts (i.e., divorce, betrayal, rape, incest, childhood pain, poverty, illness, etc.). Wearing a mask allowed us to hide and suppress our feelings as opposed to coping and healing them. To avoid the scrutiny, questions, judgment and invasion from others, women will often wear a mask, giving the impression their lives are in control.

Many women wear masks to give the appearance that they are strong, when in reality, a little girl is afraid to let the world see her cry, vulnerable or sad.

Women are socialized to help, rescue and take care of everyone else. The process of healing and taking care of ourselves is often delayed and ignored.

Men are socialized to conquer the external world and ignore the internal self. Women are socialized to be nurturers to everyone around them. Women often ignore their own care and development, resulting in feelings of resentment, stress, addictions, exhaustion, guilt, insecurity, depression and illness. After time, they realize they are feeling sick, isolated, exploited, abused, angry and burned out.

One day you can wake up realizing that you have given too much time and energy to the wrong people, the wrong activities, that you are in the wrong relationship or pursuing a career that is not compatible or satisfying. Somewhere, somehow, you lost yourself and gave your power away in exchange for love, approval, attention, acceptance or imagined power.

I have seen people make radical changes to emotionally liberate their *true self* from the bondage of being an enabler, martyr, rescuer, free counselor, pretender, crusader, protector, workaholic, cheerleader for others or doormat.

Is the "S" on your chest for Superwoman or is it for Stress? When the cape comes off: you may move to a new city, end a relationship, change careers, have a total makeover, take a long vacation, evict family members who have "stayed too long," hire a housekeeper, go to rehab, go back to school, start expressing yourself more, work fewer hours, let go of old friends, quit old bad habits.

Sometimes it's best to let everything go. Whatever is bringing you down, purge yourself of it. You'll feel a weight lifted off your back and be embraced by a sense of freedom. Are you ready to let go of old habits, unhealthy relationships, unnecessary activities, grudges and emotional baggage?

### What Is Your Emotional Temperature?

♦ Who have you given your power and peace away to?

♦ Are you feeling sick and tired of being sick and tired?

♦ Check your reflexes and responses to change or conflict.

♦ Do you have the relationship blues?

♦ Are you bored? Your boredom is in your own hands, or rather in your own brain. You must keep generating new experiences and challenges for yourself, and learn to look at old things with new eyes.

♦ Are you becoming cold, indifferent, depressed or frozen in fear?

◆ Are you slipping into the darkness of depression?

◆ Are you easily angered and impatient?

◆ Are you *crazeeee* in love and can't concentrate?

◆ Are you avoiding your life issues and escaping into a bottle, the mall, the casino, food, drugs or sleeping all the time because you can't cope?

◆ Are you feeling overwhelmed and resentful?

◆ Are you feeling centered, hopeful and peaceful as you "grow through" your life situations?

◆ Are you wearing too many masks?

**Doubt** makes decisions feel difficult, destroys your faith and causes procrastination.

**Anger** steals your peace, destroys your health and repels relationships.

**Frustration** makes you become a quitter, a whiner and stessed-out.

**Guilt** makes it impossible to enjoy any successes you achieve.

**Jealousy** creates envy, dishonesty, hate and corruption.

**A lack of emotional boundaries** allows the drama makers, controlling, demanding, needy and toxic people to consume your energy, joy, peace and time.

**Lack of exercise, a poor diet and poor rest** decrease your ability for clear thinking and good choices.

Don't be afraid. Stop talking yourself out of a blessing. You are worthy. Life is a risk. There are no guarantees. But you are guaranteed to continue living in lack and stagnation until you're ready to grow out of your comfort zone. Break the yoke of resistance, fear and procrastination. Every day miracles happen. Every day that you have breath in your body is a new beginning. Live your life expecting miracles. Live your life knowing you are blessed and that you are a blessing to others. The book of Isaiah 52 states: "Awake, clothe yourself with strength, put on garments of splendor, shake off your dust and rise up, free yourself from the chains. "Stop trippin' and wasting time with a one-sided relationship. Your head probably knows it doesn't make sense to keep trying, hoping, crying, waiting and wasting your time on someone who can't return your love. It's your heart that needs to see the truth. Your heart will keep remembering the good times and be in denial about the bad times. Too many times during my counseling sessions with clients I see someone in pain and denial only living on hope and what used to be. Even though their mate has told them they don't want to be in a committed relationship or they tell them that they are ready to move on with their life, that person sitting in the chair in my office can't let him or her go. Too many times women put their life on hold or they go into deep depression because they can't see beyond their pain, rejection and loneliness. I believe that when someone tells you or shows you who they really are, believe it. Don't deceive yourself thinking you can make someone love you or make someone stay or make someone change. Pick up the broken pieces and find yourself before you try to find someone new. Heal yourself and try to unload the emotional baggage before you carry it into a new relationship.

Congratulate yourself often on your journey to discovery and wholeness. Promise yourself to continue the healing. Teach yourself a new language. Break old habits that block your success and blessings. And continue to pray to stay strong in the spirit.

Put your life into perspective.
Things could be worse.
Count your blessings and stop the stress'n.

Haven't you seen the grace of God in your life?

You are too blessed to be stressed.

*And he said to them, "Pay attention to what you hear: the measure you give will be the measure you get, and still more will be given to you. For to those who have, more will be given; and for those who have nothing, even what they have will be taken away."*
—Mark 4:24–25

It's the way you do the things you do daily that attract or repel your success and blessings. Do you…act with impact, hide from responsibility, gossip, do what's popular, let others control your destiny, read, invest in your personal growth, sleep too much, pray, take risks, provide excellent service, neglect your health, hold grudges, practice punctuality, exercise, do just enough to get by, take shortcuts, share information, procrastinate, live and work in clutter, watch a lot of television, travel, inspire and encourage others, hate going to work, create drama, focus on creative problem solving, work on your goals, spend time with family, focus on the negative, have an attitude of gratitude and practice and strengthen your skills and talents? You become what you focus on!

*Now, brothers, I want to remind you of the gospel I preached to you, which you received and on which you have taken your stand. By this gospel you are saved, if you hold firmly to the word I preached to you. Otherwise, you have believed in vain.*

—1 Corinthians 15:1

# JOURNAL PAGE

_____

_____

_____

_____

_____

_____

_____

_____

_____

_____

# JOURNAL PAGE

_____

_____

_____

_____

_____

_____

_____

_____

_____

# JOURNAL PAGE

# CHAPTER 12

## LETTERS SENT TO THE
## SELF-ESTEEM DOCTOR

*Dear Doctor,*

=| *I have a relationship that I am not comfortable with. I am involved with someone who is married and whose wife lives abroad. I love him very much but I think that he is just sticking with me until his filing comes through. What do you think I should do? I want to get on with my life.*

—Hopeful in Miami

**Self-esteem Dr. Jewel Diamond Taylor's answer:**

You're the only one who can make the decision for yourself. You owe him nothing. You owe yourself everything. Take back your power.

Wake up from the fantasy, denial, addictive kind of love. Come on, snap out of it. Part of you wants him and part of you knows the truth. Part of you is lying to yourself and convincing you to stay. The smart part of you is God inviting you to a better way of thinking and living. I know you want love.

But you are settling for crumbs and believe me, he knows it. While you're making his life easier, you're making your life miserable.

You're living your life in a suspended hell. You're waiting and sharing your love, mind and body at his convenience. You are jeopardizing your spiritual life. Living outside of God's grace and order for your life is blocking your blessings and peace of mind.

You deserve a whole, honest and righteous man.

You have more power than you realize to determine what kind of relationship you will allow with him. You're falling, my sister. Catch yourself and stop the pain.

### Dear Doctor,

*When I was 24, I was raped by my friend's ex-husband. After that, I found it very hard to be alone with men. I haven't had a meaningful, exclusive relationship since my twenties (I'm 41 now), and though I'm ready to begin again, I'm finding it hard to meet men. What is the healthiest path for me to take when meeting a man, and how do I tell him about my past without scaring him away?*

—Ready and Willing to Love Again

### Self-esteem Dr. Jewel Diamond Taylor's answer:

Your heart and soul were raped also. Your body has healed, but your heart hasn't learned to trust. You say you are ready and willing to love again. Whether you've been raped before or not, loving someone is a risk. That violent act happened to a 24-year-old young lady. She no longer exists. The past has passed. Do you want to spend the rest of your life alone and in fear? Of course not! But as long as you continue keeping your heart closed, that "terrorist" is still stealing from you.

Take back your power. Forgive yourself if you feel any guilt, remorse or shame. Bad things do happen to good people. Things happen that we can't always protect ourselves from. You're living in a prison of fear. All men are *not* mean, ignorant, dangerous, disrespectful dogs. There are good men with good souls, respect for women and honorable intentions. Start focusing on the possibilities. Living in fear and distrust only attracts more of that into your life. You'll always see evidence and validation of your fears because that is your dominant thought and expectation. If someone appealing to you shows up in your life, know that you are worthy of love and respect. Accept lunch or dinner invitations. Proceed slowly with physical intimacy.

Trust your inner alarm system that protects you. You don't have to unload all your baggage on him right away. Your emotional baggage is not about the rape, it is about trust. If you talk about it too much or too soon, you will run a man away. If you don't talk about it, then you will be as sick as your secrets. Don't expect any relationship to be a hundred percent free of problems. Be prayerful, optimistic and courageous. If you haven't dealt with your anger, shame or depression from that emotional pain, seek out professional and spiritual guidance. Set yourself free to experience some fun, companionship, laughing, learning, sharing and the many different levels of intimacy.

You are not that 24-year-old girl anymore. You're an adult. Trust your instincts, intuition and intelligence. Give love a chance. Ready, set...grow!

## *Dear Doctor,*

*I just found out my fiancé has had intimate relations with other men. He swears this is in the past, but I'm disgusted by his admission. Is there any way we can save our relationship?*

—Jan T.

### Self-esteem Dr. Jewel Diamond Taylor's answer:

Why would you want to save a relationship that is definitely against your values, lifestyle and health? This is one reason why people lie in relationships. They have found that telling the truth leads to arguments or the end of their relationship. People learn to lie because people can't handle the truth. Denial and desperation will keep you blind, deaf and dumb. Lies about a person's sexual orientation can lead to death and divorce. If he lied and hid the truth just to keep you, one day you would wake up in your marriage feeling betrayed or with AIDS.

This man is telling you the truth *now*. He is doing you a favor. If he has those desires and tendencies, they are more than likely to continue. The question will always be in the back of your mind. Hear and accept the truth so you can set yourself free. One of my favorite quotes is, "Don't go to the altar hoping to alter your mate."

Instead of trying to save this relationship, save yourself. If you continue to convince yourself that this has to work, in essence, you are telling yourself that you don't deserve better. You would be setting yourself up for a marriage of constant mystery, distrust, jeopardizing your health, self-esteem, spiritual values and peace of mind.

I know you probably like the idea of having a fiancé. You want the wedding and you want to be a wife. But hold up. You have heard the confessions before you walked down the aisle into a life of emotional turmoil.

I know your bubble has burst. But this truth can set you free to find love again. It hurts now, but you will heal and recover from this in time. Love yourself enough to let go, so you can be free to find the right person worthy of your love, body, mind, time and trust.

## Dear Doctor,

*My partner ended his last relationship seven months ago, but I have just recently found out that his ex has been calling, and they have been talking to each other for the past few months. Do I have to put up with this? When a relationship is over, should a woman have to deal with the ex and the past?*

—plat1num2k

**Self-esteem Dr. Jewel Diamond Taylor's answer:**

Sounds like you've got a security leak in the foundation of your relationship. The alarm is sounding DANGER. What would justify your man to continue talking with his ex? Do they have a child together? Do they work together? Do they have bills and financial obligations together? A relationship can be over on many different levels.

When your partner stated it was over, he may have meant that the physical aspect of the relationship was over. He could either be still emotionally connected to his ex or he is creeping. This is your time to either ask for commitment and respect, or it's time for you to pay attention to your inner alarm system.

He could be just greedy, wanting to keep both of you. So often past lovers leave our beds but not our minds or hearts. If this continues to be an obvious intrusion and insult to the relationship that you are trying to establish, it's up to you to draw the boundary lines. He'll either stop and honor your desire for exclusivity. Or he could tell you that it's all in your imagination and there's nothing to worry about. Or he could tell you that she's just a friend and he for some reason feels responsible for her well-being and hopes you understand. Or he could tell you that he'll leave her alone and yet continue to see her in secrect. You shouldn't have to share, or constantly worry that a past relationship is stealing your joy.

If you ignore this situation, you are telling him that you feel unworthy of speaking up for yourself. You train other people how to treat you by what you say, accept, reject and what you ignore.

Don't set yourself up for heartache just because you are afraid of confrontation or afraid of losing him. This alarm could be false or real. Listen to your inner voice and you'll soon know the right thing to do. If you feel angry, betrayed or hurt, you have a right to take care of yourself and address this issue with him. If you don't, it could get out of control.

## *Dear Doctor,*

 *My husband left two years ago. I'm dating someone now who is very nice. I am a Christian and we have not become intimate yet. My husband wants to come back but he has not changed. What should I do?*
—Happy Yet Confused

**Self-esteem Dr. Jewel Diamond Taylor's answer:**

Be careful what you pray for. You wanted your husband back in your life but he has not changed (whatever that means). You are in a danger zone right now. You cannot clearly hear God's direction for your life if your heart is considering someone else. There's nothing wrong with being alone and unattached until you are more convicted about your marriage or your divorce. Everyone is nice in the beginning stages of relationships. That's just phase one. So don't get confused, my sister. You're still married.

God can't get next to you when you're about to get next to someone else to fill the emptiness of loneliness, your broken heart and your empty bed.

As your self-esteem doctor, I prescribe the following emotional vitamins for your recovery. As you read them often you will be watering the dried-up seeds of your soul. You will begin to bloom and you'll stop procrastinating on realizing your dreams and goals. This daily food will build your emotional, mental and spiritual immune system against the negativity in your life (weeds). Slowly you will recover and discover strength, courage and wisdom. Don't be too hard on yourself. Give yourself time to break the spell.

Please remember that words have power. Energy follows words. Feelings may be disguised, denied, rationalized, but a painful feeling will not go away until it has run its natural course. In fact, when a feeling is avoided, its painful effects are often prolonged and it becomes increasingly difficult to deal with it. Continually pushing down the ball of feelings only saps your energy. That ball of feelings is going to bounce back up again.

When you are honest with your feelings, you can use your energy more effectively to deal with and heal the problems.

Feel it. Deal with it. Heal it. Begin your "evolution" by reading the affirmations that follow on a regular basis.

*Teach your heart and soul a new language.*

Confidence, courage and enthusiasm
are my daily exercise.

*They said to one another, "Here comes this dreamer!"*
—Genesis 37:19

I'm ready to allow people into my life
that are supportive and nurturing.

True happiness is not in the quantity of friends, but
in their quality and support. Develop and nurture
your sanctuary of sisterhood. Through the seasons of
your life, your circle will be a place of solace to heal,
mourn, rejoice, grow, learn, laugh, play and pray.

# JOURNAL PAGE

_____

_____

_____

_____

_____

_____

_____

_____

_____

_____

# JOURNAL PAGE

# JOURNAL PAGE

_____

_____

_____

_____

_____

_____

_____

_____

_____

_____

# CHAPTER 13

## AFFIRMATIONS FOR POSITIVE LIVING

### DAILY AFFIRMATION

*This is a brand-new day...*

The past has passed. I am breathing in new health, gratitude, peace and love. I have the tenacity to solve my challenges and create my goals. I deserve respect, peace, love and the abundant life. I am not in this world alone. I know other people around me have their own pain, dreams, emotional issues, values and personal rights. I'm learning to interact and serve others with respect, integrity and compassion.

I follow through on what I start. I am worthy, loving and capable of achieving my personal definition of success. I am strong and know what I want and what I am willing to work for. My worth is not defined by my marital status, age, race, religion, job, gender, body image, income, address, car or accomplishments.

This is a brand-new day to live without apology and to live with gratitude, courage, hope, love, discernment and faith. I am growing each day with inner strength to overcome the challenges of life. I'm learning every day to forgive myself and draw emotional boundaries around those who have hurt me as I release my anger and forgive them. I am taking better care of myself. When I experience the "joy stealers" of depression, guilt, low self-esteem, clutter, fear, doubt, temptation or procrastination...I am willing to recognize and resolve my unhealthy patterns. I'm learning that all relationships are teachers. I am developing wise judgment and boundaries to know which people in my life are the lifters and which ones are the leaners.

I am using my time, talent and treasures in better ways because I realize that each day is a gift. Today I am focused on my goals and priorities because I am learning how to keep the main thing...*The Main Thing!*

I choose to live on higher ground and not drown in the sea of negativity, self-pity and unfulfillment. My life is growing in a positive new direction. I am too blessed to be stressed. I see and feel something new in myself and in those around me.

My possibilities and potential for success are unlimited. I am discovering the truth that sets me free to be more whole, relaxed, trusting, active and optimistic. I am always in the right place at the right time with the right outlook. My very presence impacts others in a positive way. I am attracting into my life people and circumstances to take my life to the next level of awareness and abundance. Those things that used to tempt and tear me apart no longer hold so much power over me because I am learning each day how to stay in the light of God's power, peace, protection, provision and a positive state of mind.

This is a brand-new day and I will be glad in it. Yes, there will be issues out of my control and yet opportunities to grow in my faith and courage. No matter what challenges or changes I must face today, this is the day the Lord has made. I am still here and there is nothing that is going to happen today that my God and I together can't handle. I will do my best to reduce my stress and until further notice...God is in charge.

Healing and transformation require: time, patience, reinforcement, commitment and repetition of good habits. To achieve results, print out then read this affirmation three times a day.

## AFFIRMATION FOR SINGLES

Yes, I am an attractive woman of intelligence and experience. I am complete whether I am married or single. I love myself and more importantly, I love the Lord.

He told me that when I delight in Him, He will give me the desires of my heart. Just because you don't see me with a mate or a date doesn't mean that I must be attracted to my same gender. I'm learning to love, appreciate and understand myself before I allow someone else in my life to appreciate the sugar I'm storing on the top shelf. I'm complete, whole and enough, whether in a relationship or not. My worth is not determined by whether I am married, divorced, single or engaged. My heavenly Father told me I'm above a diamond's worth and a gem doesn't seek, a gem is sought and cherished.

As a woman, I know it's not my role to chase after or change a man. Esther 2:1–4 states that I am to wait on my king. Since I'm learning how to cherish, value, love and honor myself, I am enjoying my life and thankful that in God's timing I will attract my divine right mate.

I am willing to heal, grow and let go of any fear or low self-esteem. I thank God for giving me the patience, discipline and self-worth to discern what and who is best suited for my time, lifestyle, standards, heart, body and soul. He will know that making love to me requires caressing my mind before caressing my body. I'm thankful for the mind and daily activities that keep me strong, active and centered in peace and satisfaction as opposed to restlessness.

I have spiritual gifts and goals to pursue. I am learning self-control to avoid the weakness of the flesh or the pressures of others and not lower my worth or values.

My divine right mate could show up in the most unexpected place or time. I will stop missing events, activities and experiences in my life just because I am single. I am taking my life's happiness out of layaway. What I am seeking is also seeking me. So I keep myself healthy, loving, active, spiritually strong and wise to become an irresistible magnet for all the good that God has in store for my life. My inner wisdom teaches me to focus on the internal vs. the external, the truth vs. denial, my heart and not just my hormones.

As I *read this affirmation daily*, I am encouraged, strengthened and empowered to radiate with wholeness, love and self-esteem. I am free of any shame, guilt, anger, grief, depression or neediness. I am loved and I am a loving person.

I realize that a great boyfriend is not necessarily the best candidate for a husband. I will give myself permission to enjoy companionship without disrespecting or neglecting my children, my health or my personal goals.

My happiness does not depend on whether or not I have a mate. My attitude of joy and completeness begins with me and my relationship with the Lord.

Even when you have put your best foot forward,
you can miss the mark…stuff happens.

You can miss your shot.

Don't beat yourself up
and count yourself out of the game.
Let go of the feelings of guilt, fear,
depression and shame.
When things don't work out, learn the lesson
and throw away the pain.

It's the way you do the things you do
that will determine your strength,
success, sanity and style.

What you think, say and do is shaping
your character and opportunities for success.

*I will instruct you and teach you in the way you should go; I will counsel you and watch over you. Do not be like the horse or the mule, which have no understanding.*

—Psalms 32: 8–9

A *whiner* feels stuck and blames others.
A **winner** is ready to make some changes.

A *whiner* has a "yes—but" attitude to all new ideas.
A **winner** is open to new ideas.

A *whiner* has a "story" to tell about her victimization. Her story becomes her identity.
A **winner** has a testimony of her endurance, deliverance, action and an "I'm gettin' up outta this" attitude.

A *whiner* feels burned out.
A **winner** feels blessed.

A *whiner* creates crises out of everything but blocks all solutions.
A **winner** seeks solutions and takes action.

A *whiner* keeps buying tickets for an emotional roller-coaster ride.
A **winner** gets out of that line and chooses to break the cycle of pain, stress, little faith, little action and limited living.

A *whiner* wishes life could get better.
A **winner** works on developing her character and goals.

A *whiner* feels like she is being punished.
A **winner** feels like she is being pushed to a new level of action, faith, strength and awareness.

A *whiner* says, "I'm tired!"
A **winner** says, "I'm inspired!"

A *whiner* says, "I can't seem to win."
A **winner** says, "I may be crying, but I won't stop trying."

A *whiner* gets discouraged easily and gives up.
A **winner** says, "I may be discouraged or delayed...but I'm never defeated. I can't give up now. I've come too far from where I started, and I know He didn't bring me this far just to leave me."

Your opportunities can come from the most unexpected places.

- ♦ **Ask** for what you want.
- ♦ **Act** on what you want.
- ♦ **Affirm** what you want.
- ♦ **Actualize** what you want.

Focus today on solutions, peace, love, right action, right speech and right thinking.
What do you want to accomplish?

Keep the main thing...*The Main Thing!*

Nobody is going to care as much about your success and "wants" in life as much as you do.

Procrastination is a passive decision to do nothing.

*Procrastination is a thief!*

- You can't win whining.
- You can't win waiting.
- You can't win weeping.
- You can't win wishing.
- Success is the result of work, endurance, commitment, discipline and passion.

I can speak up for my
rights, self-respect and
peace of mind.
I can do this!

I'm learning the difference between
being alone or feeling lonely.
I can say no or yes without guilt.
I have boundaries and values.
I do not compromise my health, time, body,
lifestyle, faith or peace of mind.
My confidence, self-esteem and inner peace
are increasing.
I am blessed. I deserve the best!

My optimism, actions, faith
and self-worth give me
motivation to continue growing
in spite of any setbacks or pain.

Today I have the strength, courage
and wisdom to endure and
enjoy my gift of life.

I am resourceful.
I am a problem solver.
I am determined to find
a way instead of finding
blame or excuses.

I believe in myself.
I believe in my dreams.
I believe I can make it.

Today…
I open my eyes to see
truth, beauty and possibilities.
I open my mind to change.
I open my heart to love.
I open my soul for healing
and peace.
I am too blessed
to be stressed!

Sometimes I win and sometimes I learn.
I live in the now with gratitude and let go of
the past as I learn the lessons they bring.

I am focused on my ways to create
my financial well-being.
My money habits, attitude and
career opportunities are improving
to increase my income, savings, freedom
and peace of mind.

## JOURNAL PAGE

_____

_____

_____

_____

_____

_____

_____

_____

_____

_____

# JOURNAL PAGE

_____

_____

_____

_____

_____

_____

_____

_____

_____

# JOURNAL PAGE

# ❧ CLOSING REMARKS ❧

You are a woman on the grow and you may feel sometimes your progress is too slow.

You may think you should have achieved more by now in this stage of your life.

You may feel overwhelmed trying to: keep up, make things work, push things through and stay on top of things at home and at work.

Stop…breathe…give yourself permission to let something go or simply say no to one more request of your time, money or peace of mind.

Continue working toward progress instead of perfection. Nothing or no one is perfect. Just keep taking steps. Continue healing your heart, mind and soul. Continue following your plan. Remain focused on your goal. Do what you have to do right now to get to the next level. Complete every task. Keep every promise and commitment. Don't look back. Stay on track. Let no one weaken your walk of faith and determination. Remain teachable. Advance by associating with achievers. Put yourself in a blessing position by associating with people who are positive. Your self-esteem and self-worth will continue to build and strengthen when you keep yourself grounded in prayer.

Something great is about to happen. I look forward to hearing your progress and praise report. Start giving thanks right now before you even see the outward manifestation of your prayers and desires. Everything you do from this day forward will put you on a journey where you will be blessed with wonderful and fruitful relationships.

*Jewel Diamond Taylor*
Founder, Women On The Grow

A volume of heartwarming devotionals
that will nourish your soul...

# NORMA DeSHIELDS BROWN

*Joy*

COMES THIS MORNING

Norma DeShields Brown's life suddenly changed
when her only son was tragically taken from her
by a senseless act. Consumed by grief, she began
an intimate journey that became
*Joy Comes This Morning.*

Filled with thoughtful devotions, Scripture readings
and words of encouragement, this powerful book
will guide you on a spiritual journey that will sustain
you throughout the years.

*Available the first week of November
wherever books are sold.*

NEW SPIRIT

™

**www.kimanipress.com**

KPNDB0351107TR

GET THE GENUINE LOVE
YOU DESERVE...

NATIONAL BESTSELLING AUTHOR
# Vikki Johnson

## *Addicted* to COUNTERFEIT LOVE

Many people in today's world are unable to recognize
what a genuine loving partnership should be and
often sabotage one when it does come along. In this
moving volume, Vikki Johnson offers memorable
words that will help readers identify destructive love
patterns and encourage them to demand the love
that they are entitled to.

*Available the first week of October wherever books are sold.*

NEW SPIRIT™

**www.kimanipress.com**

KPVJ0381007TR

*Forgiveness takes courage...*

# A MEASURE OF
# *Faith*

## MAXINE BILLINGS

With her loving husband, a beautiful home and two wonderful children, Lynnette Montgomery feels very blessed. But a sudden car accident starts a chain of events that tests her faith, and pulls to the forefront memories of a very painful childhood. At forty years of age, Lynnette comes to see that it takes a measure of faith to help one through the pains of life.

**"An enlightening read with an endearing family theme."**
**—*Romantic Times BOOKreviews***
**on *The Breaking Point***

*Available the first week of July*
*wherever books are sold.*

**www.kimanipress.com**

A soul-stirring, compelling
journey of self-discovery...

# journey
### into My Brother's Soul

*Maria D. Dowd*

Bestselling author of
*Journey to Empowerment*

A memorable collection of essays, prose and poetry,
reflecting the varied experiences that men of color face
throughout life. Touching on every facet of living—love,
marriage, fatherhood, family—these candid personal
contributions explore the essence of what it means to
be a man today.

**"*Journey to Empowerment* will lead you on a
healing journey and will lead to a great love of self,
and a deeper understanding of the many roles we
all must play in life."—*Rawsistaz Reviewers***

Coming the first week of May
wherever books are sold.

"Ms. Hudson-Smith is well-known for
her romance novels, but she will soon be
well-known for her inspirational fiction as well."
—*Rawsistaz Reviewers*

*Essence* **bestselling author**

# Linda Hudson Smith

# FIELDS *of* FIRE

### A novel

Newly engaged and working in professions
dedicated to saving lives, Stephen Trudeaux and
Darcella Coleman differ on one important decision—
whether to start a family. Then tragedy strikes and
they know it will take much reflection, faith and
soul-searching for their relationship to survive.

*Coming the first week of April,
wherever books are sold.*

Visit us at
**www.kimanipress.com**